VGM Careers for You Series

CAREERS

F O R

SCIENTIFIC TYPES
& Others with Inquiring Minds

Jan Goldberg

W9-AXZ-247

VGM Career Horizons
NTC/Contemporary Publishing Group

Library of Congress Cataloging-in-Publication Data

Goldberg, Jan.
   Careers for scientific types & others with inquiring minds / Jan Goldberg.
      p.   cm. — (VGM careers for you series)
   ISBN 0-658-00213-9 (cloth). — ISBN 0-658-00214-7 (pbk.)
   1. Science—Vocational guidance.   2. Technology—Vocational guidance.
I. Title. Careers for scientific types and others with inquiring minds.
II. Title.   III. Series.
Q147.G64   2000
502.3—dc21   99–47857
                                                                 CIP

To the memory of my beloved
parents, Sam and Sylvia
Lefkovitz, and the memory of a
dear uncle, Bernard Lefko.

Published by VGM Career Horizons
A division of NTC/Contemporary Publishing Group, Inc.
4255 West Touhy Avenue, Lincolnwood (Chicago), Illinois 60712-1975 U.S.A.
Copyright © 2000 by NTC/Contemporary Publishing Group, Inc.
Printed in the United States of America
International Standard Book Number: 0-658-00213-9 (cloth)
                                        0-658-00214-7 (paper)

00 01 02 03 04 05 LB 18 17 16 15 14 13 12 11 10 9 8 7 6 5 4 3 2 1

Contents

Acknowledgments

The author gratefully acknowledges:

- The numerous professionals who graciously agreed to be profiled in this book

- My dear husband, Larry, for his inspiration and vision

- My children—Sherri, Deborah, and Bruce—for their encouragement and love

- Family and close friends—Adrienne, Marty, Mindi, Cary, Michele, Paul, Michele, Alison, Steve, Marci, Steve, Brian, Steven, Jesse, Colin, Andrew, Bertha, and Aunt Helen—for their kindness and support

- Diana Catlin, for her insights and input

- Betsy Lancefield, editor at VGM, for making all projects rewarding and enjoyable

CHAPTER ONE

Is the Scientific Path Right for You?

Science is built up of facts, as a house is built of stones; but an accumulation of facts is not more a science than a heap of stones is a house. HENRI POINCARÉ

D id you know that for most of history, people thought that blood didn't move in the body at all? Enter William Harvey, the man who is credited with discovering the circulation of the blood. In a series of classic experiments, Harvey established the role of the heart and a modern picture of the circulatory system. As a typical experiment, he put a tourniquet on someone's arm, then, after the veins popped, pressed on them to see which direction was "downstream." This is how he discovered that blood in the veins always flows toward the heart.

In 1955 at the University of Chicago, Harold Urey and Stanley Miller performed an experiment that demonstrated how the first step in chemical evolution may have taken place. They combined methane, hydrogen, ammonia, and carbon dioxide—the materials believed to be the components of the earth's early atmosphere—and subjected the mixture to electrical sparks (thus simulating the effects of lightning). In a matter of hours they noticed that the constituents of early earth were forming molecules known as amino acids, which are the basic building blocks of proteins. In other words, Miller and Urey, starting with nonliving materials, had produced the simplest materials that make up the living cell.

In 1919, Arthur (later Sir Arthur) Eddington made what most people regard as the most dramatic and best-known confirmation of the theory of relativity. Traveling to the coast of Africa to observe a solar eclipse, he noted that the position of stars near the edge of the sun appeared to be shifted during the eclipse, a shift that could only occur if light from the stars were bent as it went around the sun.

The regularly spaced signals from a pulsar (cosmic source of pulses of radiation) look a lot like an attempt at communication from extraterrestrials. In fact, when astronomers in England first detected them in the late 1960s, they were referred to as LGM ("little green men") signals by people in the observatory.

If you find any or all of the above facts fascinating, perhaps you are a scientific type at heart. What kind of person do you need to be to most successfully enter the world of science? Take the following quiz, answering yes or no to each question. You may discover that you are, indeed, a scientific type and that one of the careers profiled within this book might be just perfect for you!

The Scientific Path—Do You Have What It Takes?

1. Do you enjoy working on long-term projects?

2. Are you a self-starter who can work alone?

3. Can you deal with "failures"—situations that don't produce the predicted result—effectively?

4. Do you have a long attention span?

5. Can you work effectively as part of a team?

6. Do you enjoy working independently on a day-to-day basis?

7. Is the idea of exploring the unknown interesting to you?

8. Do you have a strong interest in the world of science?

9. Are your math skills adequate?

10. Are you willing to earn at least a bachelor's degree?

11. Do you have strong skills in logic and problem solving?

12. Do you have a wish to be a part of something that could provide an advancement for the betterment of humanity?

Scientific types and those with inquiring minds have made incredible contributions to society since the beginnings of recorded history. Are you interested in joining that group? This book will outline a wide variety of careers that are options for you. The list is certainly not all inclusive but does provide a variety of possibilities.

Perhaps someday your name will be listed along with other scientific types mentioned in the pages of this book!

CHAPTER TWO

Careers in the Biological and Medical Sciences

The essence of science: Ask an impertinent question, and you are on the way to a pertinent answer. JACOB BRONOWSKI

W ith their inquiring minds, the following scientific types etched their names into the history books by distinguishing themselves with the following achievements: Scotsman Sir Alexander Fleming discovered penicillin in 1928; Frenchman Louis Pasteur developed germ theory in 1861; bacteria was first observed by Dutchman Antonie van Leeuwenhoek in 1683; blood circulation was discovered by Englishman William Harvey in 1619; and American Jonas Salk developed his polio vaccine in 1952.

The importance of the biological and medical sciences cannot be underestimated. For those who would consider this your calling, here's what you need to know.

Biological and Medical Scientists

Biological and medical scientists are devoted to studying living organisms and their relationships to their environments. Most of these professionals specialize in some area of biology, such as zoology (the study of animals) or microbiology (the study of microscopic organisms).

Virtually all medical scientists and many biological scientists work in the area of research and development. Some conduct basic research in an effort to increase knowledge about living organisms. Others, in applied research, use knowledge provided by basic research to develop new medicines, increase crop yields, and improve the environment. Biological and medical scientists who conduct research usually work in laboratories using electron microscopes, computers, thermal cyclers, and a wide variety of other equipment. Some professionals may conduct experiments on laboratory animals or greenhouse plants. A number of biological scientists perform a substantial amount of research outside of laboratories. For example, a botanist may do research in tropical rain forests to see what plants grow there, or an ecologist may study how a forest area recovers after a fire.

Some biological and medical scientists work in management or administration. For example, they may direct activities at zoos or botanical gardens. Some biological scientists work as consultants to business firms or to government, while others test and inspect foods, drugs, and other products or write for technical publications. Others work in sales and service jobs for companies that manufacture chemicals or other technical products.

Advances in basic biological knowledge, especially at the genetic and molecular levels, continue to spur the field of biotechnology forward. Using this technology, biological and medical scientists manipulate the genetic material of animals or plants, attempting to make organisms more productive or disease resistant. The first application of this technology occurred in the medical and pharmaceutical areas. Many substances not previously available in large quantities are now beginning to be produced by biotechnological means—some may be useful in treating cancer and other diseases. Advances in biotechnology have opened up research opportunities in almost all areas of biology, including commercial applications in agriculture and the food and chemical industries.

Most biological scientists who come under the broad category of biologist are further classified by the types of organisms they study or by the specific activities they perform, although recent advances in the understanding of basic life processes at both the molecular and cellular levels have blurred some traditional classifications.

Aquatic Biologists

Aquatic biologists study plants and animals that live in water. Marine biologists study saltwater organisms, and limnologists study freshwater organisms. Marine biologists are sometimes incorrectly called oceanographers. (Oceanography usually refers to the study of the physical characteristics of oceans and the ocean floor.)

Biochemists

Biochemists study the chemical composition of living things. They try to understand the complex chemical combinations and reactions involved in metabolism, reproduction, growth, and heredity. Much of biotechnology, which involves understanding the complex chemistry of life, is done by biochemists and molecular biologists.

Botanists

Botanists study plants and their environments. Some study all aspects of plant life; others specialize in areas such as identification and classification of plants, the structure and function of plant parts, the biochemistry of plant processes, the causes and cures of plant diseases, and the geological ancestry of plants.

Microbiologists

Microbiologists investigate the growth and characteristics of microscopic organisms such as bacteria, algae, or fungi. Medical microbiologists study the relationship between organisms and disease or the effect of antibiotics on microorganisms. Other microbiologists may specialize in environmental, food, agricultural, or industrial microbiology; virology (the study of viruses); or immunology (the study of mechanisms that fight infections). Many microbiologists use biotechnology as they advance knowledge of cell reproduction and human disease.

Physiologists

Physiologists study life functions of plants and animals under normal and abnormal conditions, both in the whole organism and at the cellular or molecular level. Physiologists may specialize in functions such as growth, reproduction, photosynthesis, respiration, or movement, or in the physiology of a certain area or system of the organism.

Zoologists

Zoologists study animals—their origins, behaviors, diseases, and life processes. Some experiment with live animals in controlled or natural surroundings, while others dissect dead animals to learn more about that species. Zoologists are usually identified by the animal group they study—for example, ornithologists (birds), mammalogists (mammals), herpetologists (reptiles and amphibians), or ichthyologists (fish).

Ecologists

Ecologists study relationships—both those among organisms and those between organisms and their environments. They also focus on the effects of influences such as population size, pollutants, rainfall, temperature, and altitude.

Medical Scientists

Biological scientists who do biomedical research are usually called medical scientists. Those working in basic research delve into the functioning of normal biological systems in order to understand the causes of and to discover treatment for diseases and other health problems. Medical scientists often try to identify the kinds of changes in a cell, chromosome, or gene that signal the development of medical problems, such as different types of cancer. After identifying structures of or changes in organisms that provide clues to health problems, medical scientists may then work on the treatment of problems.

For example, a medical scientist involved in cancer research might try to formulate a combination of drugs that will lessen the effects of the disease. Medical scientists with medical degrees might then administer those drugs to patients in clinical trials, monitor patient reactions, and observe the results. (Medical scientists who do not have medical degrees normally collaborate with the medical doctor who deals directly with patients.) The medical scientist might then return to the laboratory to examine the results and, if necessary, adjust the dosage levels to reduce negative side effects or to try to induce even better results. In addition to using basic research to develop treatments for health problems, medical scientists attempt to discover ways to prevent health problems from developing, such as affirming the link between smoking and increased risk of lung cancer, or alcoholism and liver disease.

Education and Training for Biological and Medical Scientists

Doctoral degrees are generally required for those seeking to teach at the college level and for those who wish to conduct independent research or advance to administrative positions. A master's degree is sufficient for some jobs in applied research and for jobs in management, inspection, sales, and service. A bachelor's degree is adequate for some nonresearch jobs.

Some graduates with bachelor's degrees start as biological scientists in testing and inspection or get jobs related to biological science, such as technical sales or service representatives. Occasionally, graduates with bachelor's degrees are able to work in a laboratory environment on their own projects. Some may work as research assistants. Others become biological technicians, medical laboratory technologists, or, with courses in education, high school biology teachers. Many with bachelor's degrees in biology enter medical, dental, veterinary, or other health profession schools.

Most colleges and universities offer bachelor's degrees in biological science, and many offer advanced degrees. Curriculums for advanced degrees often emphasize a subfield, such as microbiology or botany, but not all universities offer all curriculums. Advanced degree programs include classroom and fieldwork, laboratory research, and a thesis or dissertation. Biological scientists who have advanced degrees often take temporary postdoctoral research positions that provide specialized research experience.

Biological scientists need to be capable of working effectively on their own or as part of a team. In addition, they must be able to communicate clearly and concisely, both orally and in writing. Those in private industry who aspire to management or administrative positions should possess good business skills and be familiar with regulatory issues and marketing and management techniques. Those doing field research in remote areas must have physical stamina.

A doctoral (Ph.D.) degree in a biological science is the minimum education required for prospective medical scientists because that work is almost entirely research oriented. Those who possess this advanced degree are qualified to perform research on basic life processes or on particular medical problems or diseases and to analyze and interpret the results of experiments on patients. Medical scientists who administer drug or gene therapy to human patients, or who otherwise interact medically with patients (drawing blood, excising tissue, or performing other invasive procedures) must have a medical degree. It is particularly helpful for medical scientists to earn both Ph.D. and M.D. degrees.

In addition to a formal education, medical scientists are usually expected to spend several years in a postdoctoral position before they are offered permanent jobs. Postdoctoral work also provides valuable laboratory experience, including a background in specific processes and techniques (such as gene splicing) that are later transferable to other research projects. In some institutions, postdoctoral positions can lead to permanent positions.

Job Outlook

Employment of biological and medical scientists is expected to increase faster than the average for all occupations through the year 2006. Nevertheless, job seekers can expect to face considerable competition for highly sought-after basic research positions. Biological and medical scientists will continue to conduct genetic and biotechnological research and to develop and produce products derived through new biological methods.

Efforts to clean up and preserve the environment will continue to add to employment growth in these fields. More biological scientists will be needed to determine the environmental impact of industry and government actions and to correct past environmental problems. Expected expansion in research related to health issues, such as AIDS, cancer, and the Human Genome Project, should also result in growth. On the other hand, much research and development, including many areas of medical research, is funded by the federal government, and anticipated budget tightening may lead to smaller increases in research and development expenditures, further limiting the dollar amount of each grant and slowing the growth of the number of grants awarded to researchers. If, at the same time, the number of newly trained scientists continues to increase at a rate similar to that of the 1980s, both new and established scientists will experience greater difficulty winning and renewing research grants.

Biological and medical scientists are less likely to lose their jobs during recessions than those in many other occupations because most are employed on long-term research projects or in agricultural research. However, a recession could influence the amount of money allocated to new research and development efforts, particularly in areas of risky or innovative research. A recession could also limit the possibility of extension or renewal of existing projects.

Salaries for Biological and Medical Scientists

According to the National Association of Colleges and Employers, starting salaries in private industry in 1997 averaged $25,400 a year for bachelor's degree recipients in biological science, about $26,900 for master's degree recipients, and about $52,400 for doctoral degree recipients.

Median annual earnings for biological and life scientists were about $36,300 in 1996; the middle 50 percent earned between $28,400 and $50,900. Ten percent earned less than $22,000, and 10 percent earned more than $74,000.

In the federal government in 1997, general biological scientists in nonsupervisory, supervisory, and managerial positions earned an average salary of $52,100; microbiologists averaged $58,700; ecologists, $52,700; physiologists, $65,900; and geneticists, $62,700.

Parade of Professionals

Meet Amadeo J. Pesce, Ph.D.

Dr. Pesce serves as the director of the toxicology laboratory and professor of experimental medicine at the University of Cincinnati Hospital. He has been associated with the University of Cincinnati for the past twenty-three years.

"I always knew I was interested in medical research," says Dr. Pesce. "So that's where I was focused early on. I earned my undergraduate degree at the Massachusetts Institute of Technology. Then I attended Brandeis University for my graduate degree in biochemistry. My postdoctoral scholarship was at the University of Illinois at Champaign-Urbana.

"To do this kind of work, you need to have Ph.D. credentials. I also have board certification from the American Board for Clinical Chemistry, which I think is very important. Certification is given to those who have the proper scientific background, five years experience in the field, and successful completion of an examination.

"In most cases I work as part of a team of researchers. The composition of the team may change depending on the project. Participants may include postdoctoral fellows, part-time or full-time technologists, pathologists, mathematicians, psychiatrists, substance abuse counselors, and various other health and scientific professionals.

"Usually there are several projects going on at the same time. For instance, we're now helping with the clinical trials in developing methods of measurement for a couple of different projects. One project is to help pace patients by monitoring the effectiveness of the drug called AZT, which is used in the treatment of AIDS. We've developed the technology to measure the concentration of drugs inside the cell and are working very closely with the clinician and the clinical trials that are being conducted.

"Another project we're participating in is the study of developing agents that will help combat substance abuse by reducing the craving and the other aspects that make people want to continue to use drugs. In this project, we work with a group of psychiatrists and substance abuse counselors, and they provide specimens from the patients for us to monitor.

"In addition to the hours spent in the laboratory, a considerable portion of my time is spent thinking and writing. One must think things through and be able to communicate them effectively and efficiently in order for the research to have meaning. And as I convey to my students—if it's not written down, it was never done.

"As an administrator, I have other responsibilities: I supervise a postdoctoral fellow and handle personnel issues and administrative problems. And at this point in my life, I accomplish this and keep fairly regular working hours. But when I was younger (and for many years), I worked from seven in the morning until ten at night, five days a week. The other two days, I *only* worked eight to ten hours a day. This was not required, but just my own enthusiasm showing, based upon my decision to be one of the four most recognized authorities in the field. So I set on a path of learning all I could and then proceeded to put out a series of books (eighteen) about the field. This required an immense amount of work. I tell everyone that I did this to become rich and famous. My children always told me to skip the fame! But as it turns out, all I got was the fame. However, though I didn't make the money I had hoped for, it has still been very rewarding. Fans as far away as Australia have asked me to sign their copies of my books.

"This career has many other rewards—uppermost is the accomplishment of developing a theory and finding supporting data. (After all, projects are funded grants for which you must show results by a certain date in order to be funded for the next project.) On the downside, the worst part of the job is when you write a paper and it gets rejected by your peers (and you think they're wrong; in fact, you know they're wrong). However, the real issue for me is that we've done some pioneering work for people that has been fruitful and rewarding.

"Here's an example. A while back we developed a way of looking at cancer in mice, and a colleague working on cancer research sent me a letter commending me on the work and informing me of their efforts. The fact that somebody would think enough of our work to take what we've done and build on it is very rewarding.

"Another accomplishment relates to transplant patients. Some of the drugs used to treat these patients are very expensive, and we were able to devise a way of cutting the cost of those drugs from about $6,000 a year to about $1,200. This means that Third World countries can actually afford the drug for their transplant patients. That's quite an accomplishment.

"To be successful in this career, it helps to have an understanding partner, as I did. And since it is so important to be able to interact with people, exchange ideas, and get them to help with particular areas of your project, you must have the ability to get along with all kinds of people. You have to be aware of what issues others have and be able to accommodate them so they'll accommodate you in return. I have found that this is the proper approach to a successful collaboration. It's not unlike working with others on a book or any other project in which a number of people need to extend themselves in order to fulfill a common goal."

Meet H. Graham Purchase, Ph.D.

Dr. Purchase is the director of veterinary medical research at Mississippi State University.

"I was born in Rhodesia (now Zimbabwe), educated in Kenya, East Africa, and received my university training in South Africa," says Dr. Purchase. "My father, also a veterinarian who worked in research, always said that since animals feed on plants, it's wise to learn about the plant world before going to veterinary school. So I went to college when I was sixteen and earned a bachelor's degree in botany. Following this, I completed my veterinary degree in South Africa, practiced for two years, and then fulfilled my dream of coming to the United States to do research. While employed here, I earned a master's and a Ph.D. at Michigan State University (majoring in microbiology and public health). It took eight years to complete my Ph.D., but it was well worth it.

"I started my research in a poultry laboratory in East Lansing, Michigan, and after a few years, met an American girl, married her, and decided to become a citizen of the United States. I worked at the poultry research laboratory performing research on tumor viruses of poultry species for about thirteen years. And this was one occasion where I can absolutely say that I was definitely at the right place at the right time because the laboratory discovered the cause of one of the most economically devastating poultry diseases of the world (Market's disease, a form of cancer) and created a vaccine that would prevent the disease. The first commercial applicable cancer vaccine ever developed, it was initially patented and used in the United States extensively. Now it's used worldwide. This period was the most exciting and rewarding of my life.

"As a 'bench' researcher, I examined the cultures of cells in which we grew the disease-causing viruses or the vaccine that prevented the disease. Routinely I would go to the necropsy room and find those birds that had died in the experiments. I would open those birds and examine what they died from to verify that it was the challenge and not something else unrelated to the experiment. The rest of the day would involve writing up manuscripts and grant proposals. Often writing was taken home to complete because many times I couldn't get it done during the daytime hours.

"After thirteen years, I moved up into administration and was offered a job in Washington, D.C. I spent fourteen years there in nine different jobs in research administration. The research was in a variety of areas: plant, animal, human nutrition, family economics, soil, and water. But I have a great interest in veterinary research, and when the opportunity presented itself here at Mississippi State in the College of Veterinary Medicine, I took it. Here we do research on the prime commodities of Mississippi, which include one of our big income producers—catfish—and our number one product—poultry.

"As a research administrator, a typical day here involves interacting with many individuals one-on-one. I handle the budget of the college, so often there are budget forms and various commitment forms to sign—for example, allowing individuals to travel, enabling people to buy new equipment, permitting staff to be hired. There are also manuscripts and proposals to review to make sure they're suitable. We are accredited by the American Association for the Accreditation of Laboratory Animal Care, and they have very high standards of review for all experiments on animals. Every single experiment that involves animals has to be reviewed by an animal care and use committee to make sure that the animals are not harmed unnecessarily. Also the accreditation involves making sure that the facilities are maintained, so that is another area of concern for me.

"A good part of my day is devoted to meetings with my superiors to inform them about how the research projects are progressing. Frequently I have visitors to escort through our research facilities. I have reports to prepare on the research that we are doing, most of which are lay reports for general use for administrators and the legislators. The actual writing of the research itself is done by the faculty. Our system is set up so that a designated faculty member will write the proposals, then the manuscripts will be sent out for peer review to make sure that the conclusions are supported by the data, and so on. I orchestrate that review process.

"We have many levels of researchers working here. Generally speaking, the principal investigators or leaders, the ones who actually design the experiments, have doctorates. But we also have a variety of other types of careers involved. We have a lot of technicians; some have master's degrees, some have bachelor's degrees. We have animal caretakers and animal technicians; some of them have technician degrees, others are high school graduates. We have quite a number of students working toward bachelor's degrees who get some experience in the field by doing laboratory clean-up work here. Then we have graduate students and individuals who already have their bachelor's degrees who are going on to get their master's or doctorate degrees. These students spend a good deal of the time with their major professors learning how to conduct experiments and do research, so that when they graduate they'll know how to perform these tasks independently.

"If your grades are good, if you perform well during examinations, and if you can become an expert in these areas, research is a wonderful career. It's challenging and very innovative. I enjoy being able to develop something and to find out new things. But it's very rigorous, too. Most of my researchers are not here from nine to five. They're here early in the morning, they frequently miss their lunch breaks, and they take work home at night or come in at night and weekends to keep their work going. Research means pushing forward the frontiers of science, and to succeed, you must be trained, prepared, and dedicated to putting in the necessary hours and effort."

Meet Michael S. Shanler

Michael S. Shanler is an engineering research associate at the Genetics Institute, Small Molecule Drug Discovery, in Cambridge, Massachusetts.

"I received my B.S. degree in biomedical engineering from Boston University in 1996," Shanler says. "I also received Oracle OCP Database training in Boston in addition to Zymark Robotics training in Hopkington, Massachusetts. Since I am in pursuit of my M.B.A., I have also taken some business classes at Northeastern University and some biology and other science classes at Boston University.

"I began working for the Genetics Institute in March of 1997 through a temporary agency. I was then hired full-time and promoted after three months. Today, my job involves the study of preclinical drug candidates, laboratory automation, and computer modeling. The work is challenging, and I feel as if the research I do has a degree of socio-benefit.

"I suppose that perhaps I've followed in the footsteps of my father, who was an engineer with an M.B.A. I knew I wanted to earn an engineering degree but preferred something less mainstream. Hence my focus is biomedical. I entered this profession because I enjoy problem solving and want to apply what I learned in college at least for a few years before going to graduate school. After college I pursued pharmaceutical production, but I soon learned it was monotonous work, so I redirected my focus toward drug research, which is more challenging and rewarding.

"We have an enjoyable work atmosphere here. Much of my time is spent engaged in worthwhile discussions. We work hard during the week but are able to relax a bit on Fridays. The work is not dangerous, though we must use caution in working with biologicals, chemicals, and radiation. I work mostly with robotics (fifteen hours per week) and analysis of my own work (fifteen hours per week). But I'm also involved in collaborative projects and do some research/benchwork (five hours per week). The remainder of my time is spent in meetings and seminars. I can usually work about forty hours per week spending less time on some days and working through dinner on others.

"I like the uncharacteristic autonomy granted in my research position. I am held accountable for my work; however, I am free to work (or not work) my own hours, write my own protocols, and collaborate on projects. What I like least is not having a structured day, as it is too easy to be lured into taking an afternoon off.

"To others interested in entering this line of work, I would say that you shouldn't be afraid of making career-changing decisions. As soon as a job situation becomes stale, it is time to start hunting for another one. Life is too short to spend time being bored or suffering through mundane work."

Meet Dennis J. Ernst

Dennis J. Ernst is currently employed by the University of Louisville Hospital in Louisville, Kentucky. He is a medical technologist—certified by the American Society of Clinical Pathologists since 1978.

"How I got started may be broken down into two parts—what attracted me to a career in the health sciences and what attracted me to a career as a medical technologist," says Ernst. "The answers are completely different and say as much about the educational process as they do about my impatience with it.

"My mother was a registered nurse whose feelings for caring for the sick inspired me back to my earliest recollection. Because of her dedication and the satisfaction she found in her work, I came to know that caring for the sick was a noble and rewarding thing. I saw her as someone who had been blessed by fate to see and know the inner workings of the human body, and for me to be so blessed when I came of age was an intriguing prospect. In high school, the sciences enhanced my interest in health care so much that upon graduation, I enrolled in the premed program at Albion College. Incredibly, my hopes were crushed the first week. My faculty advisor called me into his office two days after I had taken the science placement exams and said that my scores did not suggest that I was likely to succeed in the rigorous premed program. Further, he said that I was poorly prepared to major in any science curriculum whatsoever. I was stunned. If I couldn't major in the sciences, I didn't want to be on this or any other campus. Nothing else interested me. Too ignorant to take his advice and too stubborn to pursue another major, I defied his wisdom and vowed to prove him and the placement tests wrong. By the time I was a junior, I had proved them only half wrong. I was majoring in biology but pulling down only mediocre grades, far below what I needed to be considered for medical school. Though the sciences continued to intrigue me, my grade point average had eliminated not only medical school, but most other high-profile careers as well. By now the struggle had been long and hard, and I was wearing thin on persistence. I had experienced enough of education but still needed to emerge with a face-saving career of some security. The allied health fields presented many offerings but most required more postgraduate study than I had the will to endure. Then my advisor recommended medical technology, the study of blood and disease. It was perfect! I could get that inside peek at the inner workings of the human body that I still craved and with only one year of postgraduate study. I applied for internships and was accepted.

"Medical technology involves the laboratory testing of body fluids and tissues for disease. This broad category consists of many subcategories. Through the years, I have worked them all in varying degrees but am currently engaged as a clinical microbiologist in a university hospital. I test blood, tissues, and body fluids for microorganisms that cause infection. I identify the microorganisms and suggest appropriate antibiotics to fight them. My work also includes immunology—the study of the presence of disease-fighting antibodies.

"I work four eight-hour days a week, enough to be considered a full-time employee. On a typical day, I begin by retrieving and collating data. This information is printed by an automated instrument that works throughout the night to identify by species the microorganisms obtained from patient cultures isolated the previous day. After identification, we determine the best antibiotic therapy against the particular organism. I enter the collated information into the hospital computer system and phone any life-threatening results to the appropriate physician for immediate treatment. Once reported, I set up newly isolated organisms for the same automated, overnight testing. Also, I am responsible for the maintenance of my automated equipment and for quality-control processes that assure my analytical systems are functioning properly.

"The work has obvious risks since one can become infected by the very organisms that are infecting the patients whom I hope to help heal. However, with the proper and consistent use of personal protective devices such as gloves, gowns, and face shields, as well as implementing safe working habits, the risk is minimal. When the hospital has many patients, the work can be quite hectic, but there are times when the patient population is low and the work is light. Often, there is not enough time in the day to complete all of my responsibilities. Since overtime is not allowed in our laboratory, any time spent working more than the hours scheduled must be offset by working proportionally less another day.

"Nearly all of my coworkers have either associate's or bachelor's degrees, and all are certified laboratory professionals in one capacity or another. The laboratory assistants who prepare the specimens for bacterial isolation and perform a multitude of nontechnical tasks are high school graduates who have received on-the-job training. The level of cooperation among us is high, as is our goal-oriented momentum. Rarely does a day pass when someone doesn't ask me if I need any help. This is the most satisfying aspect of my work.

"Anyone interested in a career in the allied health sciences should consider medical technology for the insights it offers into the inner workings of the human body. Here one finds the constant discovery of the body's beauty and complexity that I hungered for as the young, observant son of a nurse. The intrigue has never ceased. Applications of the skills learned in training are many and varied, rendering the possibility of job burnout in this career remote. However, because of the sweeping application of managed-care strategies in health care today, medical technology as a career has transformed from one of promised permanence to one that is, at best, a stepping-stone to a more secure and respected calling."

For More Information

For information on careers in the biological sciences, contact:

American Institute of Biological Sciences
1444 I Street NW, Suite 200
Washington, DC 20005
Homepage: http://www.aibs.org

For information on careers in physiology, contact:

American Physiological Society
Education Office
9650 Rockville Pike
Bethesda, MD 20814
Homepage: http://www.faseb.org/aps

For information on careers in biotechnology, contact:

Biotechnology Industry Organization
1625 K Street NW, Suite 1100
Washington, DC 20006

For information on careers in biochemistry, contact:

American Society for Biochemistry and Molecular Biology
9650 Rockville Pike
Bethesda, MD 20814

For information on careers in biophysics, contact:

Biophysical Society
9650 Rockville Pike, Room 0512
Bethesda, MD 20814

For information on careers in botany, contact:

Botanical Society of America
Business Office
1735 Neil Avenue
Columbus, OH 43210
Homepage: http://www.botany.org

For information on careers in microbiology, contact:

American Society for Microbiology
Office of Education and Training—Career Information
1325 Massachusetts Avenue NW
Washington, DC 20005
Homepage: http://www.asmusa.org

Information on acquiring a job as a biological or medical scientist with the federal government may be obtained from the Office of Personnel Management through a telephone-based system. Consult your telephone directory under U.S. Government for a local number or visit the website at http://www.usajobs.opm.gov.

CHAPTER THREE

Careers in the Physical Sciences

Lucky is he who has been able to understand the causes of things. VIRGIL

D id you know that studying balloons can lead to great discoveries? Have you ever heard of Charles's law? It states that the volume of a given mass of gas at constant pressure is directly proportional to its absolute temperature (in kelvin). The law is attributed to the work of Jacques Charles (1746–1823), a French physicist who studied gases and made his first ascent in a hydrogen-filled balloon in 1783. Upon hearing about the hot-air balloons of the French Montgolfier brothers, Charles and his brothers began experimenting with hydrogen balloons. Incredibly, they made their ascent only ten days after the Montgolfiers' first flight. Charles's work on the expansion of gases led to the formulation of the 1787 law that bears his name.

True Investigators

Physical scientists serve as investigators, continually involved in a never-ending search to learn more about the laws that govern our universe.

Chemists

A chemist's goal is to search for new knowledge about chemicals and put it to practical use. Although chemicals are often thought of as artificial or toxic substances, all physical things, whether naturally occurring or of human design, are composed of chemicals. Chemists have developed a tremendous variety of new and improved synthetic fibers: paints, adhesives, drugs, cosmetics, electronic components, lubricants, and thousands of other products. They also develop processes that save energy and reduce pollution, such as improved oil refining and petrochemical processing methods. Research on the chemistry of living things spurs advances in medicine, agriculture, food processing, and other areas.

Many chemists work in research and development. In basic research, chemists investigate the properties, composition, and structure of matter and the laws that govern the combination of elements and reactions of substances. In applied research and development, they create new products and processes or improve existing ones, often using knowledge gained from basic research. For example, synthetic rubber and plastics resulted from research on small molecules uniting to form large ones (polymerization).

Chemists also work in production and quality control in chemical manufacturing plants. They prepare instructions that specify ingredients, mixing times, and temperatures for each stage in the process. They also monitor automated processes to ensure proper product yield, and they test samples to ensure they meet industry and government standards. Chemists also record and report on test results. Some serve as marketing or sales representatives who sell and provide technical information on chemical products.

Chemists often specialize in a subfield. For instance, analytical chemists determine the structure, composition, and nature of substances and develop analytical techniques. They also identify the presence and concentration of chemical pollutants in air, water, and soil. Organic chemists study the chemistry of the vast number of carbon compounds. Many commercial products, such as drugs, plastics, and fertilizers, have been developed by organic chemists. Inorganic chemists study compounds consisting mainly of elements other than carbon, such as those in electronic components. Physical chemists study the characteristics of atoms and molecules and investigate how chemical reactions work. Their research may result in new and better energy sources.

Chemists who work in production and quality control test samples to ensure that product specifications are met.

Physicists and Astronomers

Physicists explore and identify basic principles governing the structure and behavior of matter, the generation and transfer of energy, and the interaction of matter and energy. Some physicists use these principles in theoretical areas, such as the nature of time and the origin of the universe; others apply their physics knowledge to practical areas, such as the development of advanced materials, electronic and optical devices, and medical equipment.

Physicists design and perform experiments with lasers, cyclotrons, telescopes, mass spectrometers, and other equipment. Based on observation and analysis, they attempt to discover the laws that describe the forces of nature, such as gravity, electromagnetism, and nuclear interactions. They also find ways to apply physical laws and theories to problems in nuclear energy, electronics, optics, materials, communications, aerospace technology, navigation equipment, and medical instrumentation.

Most physicists work in research and development. Some do basic research to increase scientific knowledge. Physicists who conduct applied research build upon the discoveries made through basic research and work to develop new devices, products, and processes. For instance, basic research in solid-state physics led to the development of transistors and then to the integrated circuits used in computers.

Physicists also design research equipment that often has additional unanticipated uses. For example, lasers are used in surgery; microwave devices are used for ovens; and measuring instruments can analyze blood or the chemical content of foods. A small number of physicists work in inspection, testing, quality control, and other production-related jobs in industry.

Much physics research is done in small or midsize laboratories. However, experiments in plasma, nuclear energy, high energy, and some other areas of physics require extremely large, expensive equipment, such as particle accelerators. Physicists in these subfields often work in large teams. Although physics research may require extensive experimentation in laboratories, research physicists still spend time in offices planning, recording, analyzing, and reporting on research.

Physicists generally specialize in one of many subfields— elementary particle physics; nuclear physics; atomic and molecular physics; physics of condensed matter (solid-state physics); optics; acoustics; plasma physics; or the physics of fluids. Some specialize in a subdivision of one of these subfields; for example, within condensed matter physics, specialties include superconductivity, crystallography, and semiconductors. However, since all areas of physics involve the same fundamental principles, specialties may overlap, and physicists may switch from one subfield to another. Also, growing numbers of physicists work in combined fields such as biophysics, chemical physics, and geophysics.

Astronomy

Astronomy is sometimes considered a subfield of physics because astronomers use the principles of physics and mathematics to learn about the fundamental nature of the universe, including the sun, moon, planets, stars, and galaxies. They also apply their knowledge to problems in navigation and space flight.

Almost all astronomers do research. They analyze large quantities of data gathered by observatories and satellites and write scientific papers or reports on their findings. Most astronomers spend only a few weeks each year making observations with optical telescopes, radio telescopes, and other instruments. Contrary to the popular image, astronomers almost never make observations by looking directly through a telescope because enhanced photographic and electronic detecting equipment can see more than the human eye.

Geologists and Geophysicists

Geologists and geophysicists, also known as geological scientists or geoscientists, study the physical aspects and history of the earth. They identify and examine rocks, study information collected by remote sensing instruments in satellites, conduct geological surveys, construct maps, and use instruments to measure the earth's gravity and magnetic field. They also analyze information collected through seismic studies, which involves bouncing energy waves off buried rock layers. Many geologists and geophysicists search for oil, natural gas, minerals, and groundwater.

Other geological scientists play an important role in preserving and cleaning up the environment. Their activities include designing and monitoring waste disposal sites, preserving water supplies, and reclaiming contaminated land and water to comply with federal environmental regulations. They also help locate safe sites for hazardous waste facilities and landfills.

Geologists and geophysicists examine chemical and physical properties of specimens in laboratories. They study fossil remains of animal and plant life or experiment with the flow of water and oil through rocks. Geoscientists sometimes use two- or three-dimensional computer modeling to portray water layers and the flow of water or other fluids through rock cracks and porous materials. They use a variety of sophisticated laboratory instruments, including x-ray diffractometers, which determine the crystal structure of minerals, and petrographic microscopes, for the study of rock and sediment samples. Geoscientists also use seismographs, instruments that measure energy waves resulting from movements in the earth's crust, to determine the locations and intensities of earthquakes.

Geoscientists working in the oil and gas industry sometimes process and interpret the maps produced by remote-sensing satellites to help identify potential new oil or gas deposits. Seismic technology is another important exploration tool. Seismic waves are used to develop three-dimensional computer models of underground or underwater rock formations.

Geologists and geophysicists also apply geological knowledge to engineering problems in constructing large buildings, dams, tunnels, and highways. Some administer and manage research and exploration programs; others become general managers in petroleum and mining companies.

Geology and geophysics are closely related fields, but there are major differences. Geologists study the composition, structure, and history of the earth's crust. They try to find out how rocks were formed and what has happened to them since their formation. Geophysicists use the principles of physics and mathematics to study not only the earth's surface but its internal composition, ground and surface waters, atmosphere, and oceans as well as its magnetic, electrical, and gravitational forces. Both, however, commonly apply their skills to the search for natural resources and to solve environmental problems.

There are numerous subdisciplines or specialties under the two major disciplines of geology and geophysics that further differentiate the kind of work geoscientists do. For example, petroleum geologists explore for oil and gas deposits by studying and mapping the subsurface of the ocean or land. They use sophisticated geophysical instrumentation and computers to collect information. Mineralogists analyze and classify minerals and precious stones according to composition and structure. Paleontologists study fossils found in geological formations to trace the evolution of plant and animal life and the geologic history of the earth. Stratigraphers help to locate minerals by studying the distribution and arrangement of sedimentary rock layers and by examining the fossil and mineral content of such layers. Those who study marine geology are usually called oceanographers or marine geologists. They study and map the ocean floor and collect information using remote-sensing devices aboard surface ships or underwater research craft.

Geophysicists may specialize in areas such as geodesy, seismology, or marine geophysics, also known as physical oceanography. Geodesists study the size and shape of the earth, its gravitational field, tides, polar motion, and rotation. Seismologists interpret data from seismographs and other geophysical instruments to detect earthquakes and locate earthquake-related faults. Physical oceanographers study the physical aspects of oceans, such as currents and the interaction of sea surface and atmosphere.

Hydrology is a discipline closely related to geology and geophysics. Hydrologists study the distribution, circulation, and physical properties of underground and surface waters. They study the form and intensity of precipitation, its rate of infiltration into the soil, its movement through the earth, and its return to the ocean and atmosphere. The work they do is particularly important in environmental preservation and remediation.

Meteorologists

Meteorology is the study of the atmosphere, the air that covers the earth. Meteorologists study the atmosphere's physical characteristics, motions, and processes, and the way the atmosphere affects the rest of our environment. The best-known application of this knowledge is in forecasting the weather. However, weather information and meteorological research also are applied in air-pollution control, agriculture, air and sea transportation, defense, and the study of trends in the earth's climate, such as global warming or ozone depletion.

Meteorologists who forecast the weather, known professionally as operational meteorologists, are the largest group of specialists. They study information on air pressure, temperature, humidity, and wind velocity, and they apply physical and mathematical relationships to make short- and long-range weather forecasts. Their data come from weather satellites, weather radar, and remote sensors and observers in many parts of the world. Meteorologists use sophisticated computer models of the world's atmosphere to make long-term, short-term, and local forecasts. These forecasts inform not only the general public but also those who need accurate weather information for both economic and safety reasons, as in the shipping, aviation, agriculture, fishing, and utilities industries.

The use of weather balloons, launched several times a day, to measure wind, temperature, and humidity in the upper atmosphere is supplemented by far more sophisticated weather equipment that transmits data as frequently as every few minutes. Doppler radar, for example, can detect rotational patterns in violent storm systems, allowing forecasters to better predict thunderstorms, tornadoes, and flash floods, as well as their direction and intensity.

Some meteorologists work in research. Physical meteorologists, for example, study the atmosphere's chemical and physical properties; the transmission of light, sound, and radio waves; and the transfer of energy in the atmosphere. They also study factors affecting formation of clouds, rain, snow, and other weather phenomena, such as severe storms. Climatologists collect, analyze, and interpret past records of wind, rainfall, sunshine, and temperature in specific areas or regions. Their studies are used to design buildings and to plan heating and cooling systems, to aid in effective land use, and in agricultural production. Other research meteorologists examine the most effective ways to control or diminish air pollution or improve weather forecasting using mathematical models.

Jobs in weather stations, most of which operate around the clock seven days a week, often involve night, weekend, and holiday work and rotating shifts. During times of weather emergencies, such as hurricanes, operational meteorologists may work overtime. Operational meteorologists are also often under pressure to meet forecast deadlines. Weather stations are found all over the country: in airports, in or near cities, and in isolated and remote areas.

Some meteorologists also spend time observing weather conditions and collecting data from aircraft. Meteorologists in smaller weather offices often work alone. Sometimes, those working in larger offices work as members of a team. Meteorologists not involved in forecasting work regular hours, usually in offices. Those who work for private consulting firms or for companies that analyze and monitor emissions to improve air quality often work with other science or engineering professionals.

Education and Training

Chemists

A bachelor's degree in chemistry or a related discipline is usually the minimum education necessary to work as a chemist. However, many, if not most, research jobs require a doctoral degree.

Many colleges and universities offer bachelor's degree programs in chemistry, and a large number are approved by the American Chemical Society. Several hundred colleges and universities also offer advanced degree programs in chemistry.

Students planning careers as chemists should enjoy studying science and mathematics and should like working with their hands building scientific apparatus and performing experiments. In addition to required courses in analytical, inorganic, organic, and physical chemistry, undergraduate chemistry majors usually study biological sciences, mathematics, and physics. Computer courses are invaluable, as employers increasingly prefer job applicants to be not only computer literate but able to apply computer skills to modeling and simulation tasks. Laboratory instruments are also computerized, and the ability to operate and understand equipment is a necessity. Perseverance, curiosity, and the ability to concentrate on detail and to work independently are also essential.

Because chemists who engage in research and development are increasingly expected to work on interdisciplinary teams, some understanding of other disciplines, including business and marketing or economics, is desirable, along with leadership ability and good oral and written communication skills. Experience, either in academic laboratories or through internships or co-op programs in industry, also is useful. Some employers of research chemists, particularly in the pharmaceutical industry, prefer to hire individuals with several years of postdoctoral experience.

Although graduate students typically specialize in a subfield of chemistry, such as analytical chemistry or polymer chemistry, students usually need not specialize at the undergraduate level. In fact, undergraduates who are broadly trained have more flexibility when job hunting or changing jobs than if they narrowly define their interests. Most employers provide new bachelor's degree chemists with additional training or education.

In government or industry, beginning chemists with bachelor's degrees work in technical sales or services, quality control, or assist senior chemists in research and development laboratories. Some may work in research positions, analyzing and testing products, but these may be technicians' positions, with limited upward mobility. Many employers prefer chemists with doctorates to work in basic and applied research. A doctorate is also generally preferred for advancement to many administrative positions. Chemists who work in sales, marketing, or professional research positions often eventually move into management.

Many people with bachelor's degrees in chemistry enter other occupations in which a chemistry background is helpful, such as technical writing or chemical marketing. Some enter medical, dental, veterinary, or other health profession schools.

Chemistry graduates may also become high school teachers, and those with doctorates may teach at the college or university level. However, they usually are then regarded as science teachers or college or university professors rather than as chemists. Others may qualify as engineers, especially if they have taken some courses in engineering.

Physicists and Astronomers

Because most jobs are in research and development, a doctoral degree is the usual educational requirement for physicists and astronomers. Many physics and astronomy doctorate holders ultimately take jobs teaching at the college or university level. Additional experience and training in a postdoctoral research assignment, although not required, is helpful in preparing physicists and astronomers for permanent research positions.

Those having bachelor's or master's degrees in physics are rarely qualified to fill positions as physicists. They are, however, usually qualified to work in engineering-related or other scientific fields as technicians or to assist in setting up laboratories. Some may qualify for applied research jobs in private industry or nonresearch positions in the federal government. A master's degree often suffices for teaching jobs in two-year colleges. Those with bachelor's degree in astronomy often enter an unrelated field, but they are also qualified to work in planetariums running science shows or to assist astronomers doing research.

Hundreds of colleges and universities offer bachelor's degrees in physics. The undergraduate program provides a broad background in the natural sciences and mathematics. Typical physics courses include mechanics, electromagnetism, optics, thermodynamics, atomic physics, and quantum mechanics.

About 180 colleges and universities offer doctoral degrees in physics. Graduate students usually concentrate in a subfield of physics, such as elementary particles or condensed matter. Many begin studying for their doctorate immediately after earning their bachelor's degrees.

About forty universities offer a doctoral degree in astronomy, either through an astronomy department, a physics department, or a combined physics/astronomy department. Applicants to astronomy doctoral programs face keen competition for available slots. Those planning a career in astronomy should have a very strong physics background. In fact, an undergraduate degree in physics is excellent preparation for a doctorate in astronomy.

Mathematical ability, computer skills, an inquisitive mind, imagination, and the ability to work independently are important traits for anyone planning a career in physics or astronomy. Prospective physicists who hope to work in industrial laboratories applying physics knowledge to practical problems should broaden their educational backgrounds to include courses outside of physics, such as economics, computer technology, and current affairs. Good oral and written communication skills are also important because many physicists work as part of a team or have contact with persons with nonphysics backgrounds, such as clients or customers.

The beginning job for most physics and astronomy doctoral graduates is conducting research in a postdoctoral position, where they may work with experienced physicists as they continue to learn about their specialties and develop ideas and results to be used in later work. The initial work may be routine and remain under the close supervision of senior scientists. After some experience, they perform more complex tasks and work more independently. Physicists who develop new products or processes sometimes form their own companies or join new firms to exploit their own ideas.

Geophysicists

A bachelor's degree in geology or geophysics is adequate for entry into some lower-level geology jobs, but better jobs with good advancement potential usually require at least a master's degree in geology or geophysics. Persons with strong backgrounds in physics, chemistry, mathematics, or computer science also may qualify for some geophysics or geology jobs. A Ph.D. is required for most research positions in colleges and universities, and is also important for work in federal agencies and some state geological surveys that involve basic research.

Hundreds of colleges and universities offer a bachelor's degree program in geology, geophysics, oceanography, or other geosciences. Other programs offering related training for beginning geological scientists include geophysical technology, geophysical engineering, geophysical prospecting, engineering geology, petroleum geology, hydrology, and geochemistry. In addition, several hundred more universities award advanced degrees in geology or geophysics.

It is important for geologists and geophysicists to be capable of working as part of a team. Computer modeling, data processing, and effective oral and written communication skills are important, as well as the ability to think independently and creatively. Those involved in fieldwork must have physical stamina.

Traditional geoscience courses emphasizing classical geologic methods and topics (such as mineralogy, paleontology, stratigraphy, and structural geology) are important for all geoscientists. However, those students interested in working in the environmental or regulatory fields should take courses in hydrology, hazardous waste management, environmental legislation, chemistry, mechanics, and geologic logging. Also, some employers seek applicants with field experience, so a summer internship or employment in an environmentally related area may be beneficial to prospective geoscientists.

Geologists and geophysicists often begin their careers in field exploration or as research assistants in laboratories. As they gain experience, they are given more difficult assignments. Eventually they may be promoted to project leader, program manager, or another management or research position.

Meteorologists

A bachelor's degree with a major in meteorology or a closely related field with course work in meteorology is the usual minimum requirement for a beginning job as a meteorologist.

The preferred educational requirement for entry-level meteorologists in the federal government is a bachelor's degree, not necessarily in meteorology, with at least twenty semester hours of meteorology courses, including six hours in weather analysis and forecasting and six hours in dynamic meteorology. In addition to meteorology course work, differential and integral calculus and six hours of college physics are required. These requirements have recently been upgraded to include course work in computer science and additional course work appropriate for a physical science major, such as statistics, chemistry, physical oceanography, or physical climatology. Sometimes, a combination of experience and education may be substituted for a degree.

Although positions in operational meteorology are available for those with only a bachelor's degree, obtaining a graduate degree enhances advancement potential. A master's degree is usually necessary for conducting research and development, and a doctorate may be required for some research positions. Students who plan a career in research and development need not necessarily major in meteorology as undergraduates. In fact, a bachelor's degree in mathematics, physics, or engineering is excellent preparation for graduate study in meteorology.

Because meteorology is a small field, relatively few colleges and universities offer degrees in meteorology or atmospheric science, although many departments of physics, earth science, geography, and geophysics offer atmospheric science and related courses. Prospective students should make certain that courses required by the National Weather Service and other employers are offered at the college they are considering. Computer science courses, additional meteorology courses, and a strong background in mathematics and physics are important to prospective employers. Many programs combine the study of meteorology with another field, such as agriculture, engineering, or physics. For example, hydrometeorology is the blending of hydrology (the science of the earth's water) and meteorology, and is the field concerned with the effect of precipitation on the hydrologic cycle and the environment.

Beginning meteorologists often do routine data collection, computation, or analysis and some basic forecasting. Entry-level meteorologists in the federal government are usually placed in intern positions for training and experience. Experienced meteorologists may advance to various supervisory or administrative jobs or may handle more complex forecasting jobs. Increasing numbers of meteorologists establish their own weather consulting services.

Job Outlook

Chemists

Employment of chemists is expected to grow about as fast as the average for all occupations through the year 2006. The chemical industry, the major employer of chemists, should face continued demand for goods, such as new and better pharmaceuticals and personal care products, as well as more specialty chemicals designed to address specific problems or applications. To meet these demands, research and development expenditures in the chemical industry will continue to increase, contributing to employment opportunities for chemists.

Within the chemical industry, job opportunities are expected to be most plentiful in pharmaceutical and biotechnology firms. Stronger competition among drug companies and an aging population are among the several factors contributing to the need for innovative and improved drugs discovered through scientific research. Although employment growth is expected to be slower in the remaining segments of the chemical industry, there will still be a need for chemists to develop and improve products, such as cosmetics and cleansers, as well as the technologies and processes used to produce chemicals for all purposes. Job growth will also be spurred by the need for chemists to monitor and measure air and water pollutants to ensure compliance with local, state, and federal environmental regulations.

Because much employment growth of chemists is expected to relate to drug research and development and environmental issues, analytical, environmental, and synthetic organic chemists should have the best job prospects.

During periods of economic recession, layoffs of chemists may occur—especially in the oil refining and industrial chemicals industries. Chemists are vulnerable to temporary slowdowns in automobile manufacturing and construction, end users of many of the products of the chemical industry.

Physicists and Astronomers

A large proportion of physicists and astronomers are employed on research projects, many of which, in the past, were defense related. Expected reductions in defense-related research and an expected slowdown in the growth of civilian physics-related research will cause employment of physicists and astronomers to experience a small decline through the year 2006. Proposed employment cutbacks and overall budget tightening in the federal government will also affect employment of physicists, especially those dependent on federal research grants. The number of doctorates granted in physics has been much greater than the number of openings for physicists for several years. Although physics enrollments are starting to decline slightly, the number of new Ph.D. graduates is likely to continue to be high enough to result in keen competition for the kind of research and academic jobs that those with new doctorates in physics have traditionally sought. Also, more prospective researchers will likely compete for less grant money.

Although research and development budgets in private industry will continue to grow, many research laboratories in private industry are expected to reduce basic research, which is where much physics research takes place, in favor of applied or manufacturing research and product and software development. Furthermore, although the median age of physicists and astronomers is higher than the average for all occupations and many will be eligible for retirement in the next decade, it is possible that many of them will not be replaced when they retire.

Those with only a bachelor's degree in physics or astronomy are not qualified to enter most physicist or astronomer jobs. However, many find jobs as high school physics teachers and in engineering, technician, mathematics, and computer and environment-related occupations. Despite the strong competition for, and expected employment declines in, traditional physics and astronomical research oriented jobs, individuals with a physics degree at any level will find their skills useful for entry to many other occupations.

Geologists and Geophysicists

Many jobs for geologists and geophysicists are in or related to the petroleum industry, especially the exploration for oil and gas. This industry is subject to cyclical fluctuations. Low oil prices, higher production costs, improvements in energy efficiency, shrinking oil reserves, and restrictions on potential drilling sites have caused exploration activities to be curtailed in the United States. If these conditions continue, there will be limited openings in the petroleum industry for geoscientists working in the United States.

As a result of generally poor job prospects in the past few years, the number of students enrolling in geology and geophysics has dropped considerably. Although enrollments are rising again, the number of students trained in petroleum geology is likely to be so low that even a small increase in openings in the oil industry will be greater than the number of petroleum geologists and geophysicists available to fill them, creating good employment opportunities if exploration activities increase significantly. Employment prospects will be best for job seekers who hold a master's degree and are familiar with the advanced technologies, such as computer modeling, which are increasingly used to locate new oil and gas fields or pinpoint hidden deposits in existing fields. Because of the cyclical nature of the oil and gas industry, hiring on a contractual basis is common.

Despite the generally poor job prospects encountered by geoscientists in recent years in the petroleum industry, employment of geologists and geophysicists is expected to grow as fast as the average for all occupations through the year 2006. Recent setbacks have been offset by increased demand for these professionals in environmental protection and reclamation and the generally improved outlook in the oil and gas industry. Geologists and geophysicists will continue to be needed to help clean up contaminated sites in the United States and to help private companies and government comply with more numerous and complex environmental regulations. In particular, jobs requiring training in engineering geology, hydrology, and geochemistry should be in demand. However, the number of geoscientists obtaining training in these areas has been increasing, so competition may increase despite the growing number of jobs available.

Meteorologists

Persons seeking employment as meteorologists are likely to face competition because the National Weather Service, the largest single employer of meteorologists, has curtailed hiring following an extensive modernization of its weather forecasting equipment.

As a whole, employment of meteorologists is expected to grow more slowly than the average for all occupations through the year 2006. Employment of meteorologists in other parts of the federal government is not expected to increase either. Some employment growth is anticipated in private industry as the use of private weather forecasting and meteorological services by farmers, commodity investors, utilities, transportation and construction firms, and radio and television stations increases. For people in these and other areas, additional weather information, which is more closely targeted to their needs than the more general information provided by the National Weather Service, can yield significant benefits. However, because many private weather service customers are in industries sensitive to fluctuations in the economy, the sales and growth of private weather services depend on the health of the economy.

There will continue to be demand for meteorologists to analyze and monitor the dispersion of pollutants into the air to ensure compliance with the federal environmental regulations outlined in the Clean Air Act of 1990.

Salaries

Chemists

A survey by the American Chemical Society reports that the median salary of all their members with bachelor's degrees was $49,400 a year in 1997; with master's degrees, $56,200; and with doctorates, $71,000. Median salaries were highest for those working in private industry; those in academia earned the least. According to an ACS survey of recent graduates, inexperienced chemistry graduates with bachelor's degrees earned a median starting salary of $25,000 in 1996; with master's degrees, $31,100;

and with doctorates, $45,000. Among bachelor's degree graduates, those who had completed internships or had other work experience while in school commanded the highest starting salaries. In 1997, chemists in nonsupervisory, supervisory, and managerial positions in the federal government earned an average salary of $60,000.

Physicists and Astronomers

The American Institute of Physics reported a median salary of $65,000 in 1996 for members with doctorates; with master's degrees, $55,000; with bachelor's degrees, $50,000. Those working in temporary postdoctoral positions earned significantly less.

Average earnings for physicists in nonsupervisory, supervisory, and managerial positions in the federal government in 1997 were $71,800 a year; for astronomy and space scientists, $77,400.

According to a 1997 National Association of Colleges and Employers survey, the average starting salary offer to physics doctoral degree candidates was $63,000.

Geologists and Geophysicists

Surveys by the National Association of Colleges and Employers indicate that graduates with bachelor's degrees in geology and the geological sciences received an average starting offer of about $30,900 a year in 1997. However, the starting salaries can vary widely, depending on the employing industry. For example, according to a 1996 American Association of Petroleum Geologists survey, the average salary in the oil and gas industry for geoscientists with less than two years of experience was about $48,400.

Although the petroleum, mineral, and mining industries offer higher salaries, competition in these areas is normally intense, and the job security less than in other areas.

In 1997, the federal government's average salary for geologists in managerial, supervisory, and nonsupervisory positions was $59,700; for geophysicists, $67,100; for hydrologists, $54,800; and for oceanographers, $62,700.

Meteorologists

The average salary for meteorologists in nonsupervisory, supervisory, and managerial positions employed by the federal government was $57,000 in 1997. In 1995, meteorologists in the federal government with bachelor's degrees and no experience received starting salaries between $19,500 and $24,200 a year, depending on their college grades. Those with master's degrees could start at $24,200 to $29,600; those with doctorates started at $35,800 to $42,900. Beginning salaries for all degree levels were slightly higher in selected areas of the country where the prevailing local pay level was higher.

Parade of Professionals

Meet Sara Sawtelle, Ph.D.

Dr. Sara Sawtelle serves as the manager of technical services at Environmental Test Systems, Inc., in Elkhart, Indiana. ETS was founded in 1985 to develop consumer and industrial applications for reagent strip technology. Test strips have been widely used in the medical diagnostic industry since the 1960s, when their introduction revolutionized the way physicians performed urinalysis and blood tests. The company has adapted the technology for applications in such diverse fields as pool and spa water testing, drinking water quality testing, automobile and diesel truck coolant testing, and industrial in-process testing. Research and development efforts are ongoing as scientists continuously explore a variety of potential applications for the test strip.

"I was attracted to chemistry because of all the interesting things that are part of chemistry," Dr. Sawtelle says. "The more I learned, the more intrigued I became with how chemistry and life were connected. So, I pursued my education and focused in science.

"I earned my B.S. in science (with a major in chemistry) from Clarion University of Pennsylvania in 1988. Subsequently, I earned my Ph.D. in analytical chemistry from Boston College in Chestnut Hill, Massachusetts, in 1992.

"I started here in my present position on May 12, 1997. Environmental Test Systems was looking for a chemist with good communication and people skills. At the time, I was teaching at a local college while seeking an area position that would let me make use of the parts of teaching that I enjoy, while omitting the parts I did not. This position does just that!

"My job does not have a typical day. I am very busy but not over-stressed. I work forty-plus hours per week in an atmosphere that is very team oriented. As a member of technical services, I am a part of the marketing department. This enables me to share the joy of chemistry with others, particularly nonchemists. I find the interactions intriguing and usually come away learning more all the time. It is also an environment that encourages 'out of the box' thinking—one in which we are encouraged to grow and learn. I assist customers with technical questions, acting as the technical liaison between the lab and the marketing department. I spend time talking with customers about our products, learn about new products that are coming out, and help in the legwork of marketing and developing a new product.

"I really enjoy working in this environment. The strength of this company is that from the president down to the line worker, everyone is considered important and has an invaluable function. It is a nice atmosphere in which to thrive.

"The most difficult part of the job is working with difficult customers. But this is to be expected. Still, the hard part is not letting them get to you so that you join them in their attitude.

"Most of my job centers around communication—communication within the company, communication between scientists and nonscientists, communication externally with customers explaining 'problems' to them in lay terms. Communication is also of the utmost importance to presentations that are given to professionals in the fields that use our products.

"My previous experience teaching chemistry at the college level for five years has been very valuable in this undertaking. Among other things, it taught me how to listen and not jump to conclusions about what a person may be asking.

"My advice is to believe in yourself and to not try to be someone else. Don't try to change who you are. And don't expect that the job you get out of college or school will be 'the job' for you. As you grow as a person, you should be willing to try new things or new career paths. I never thought I would be where I am. I expected to become a college professor. But once I tried it, I found that there were aspects of the profession that did not work for me. I like being in the position I am. So I guess my advice is to make sure you like your career—or it is just not worth your energy. If you don't like it—move on."

Meet Ken Rubin, Ph.D.

Dr. Rubin serves as assistant professor on the staff of the University of Hawaii in the Department of Geology and Geophysics, School of Ocean and Earth Science and Technology (SOEST).

"I earned my B.A. from the University of California at San Diego in chemistry in 1984," says Dr. Rubin. "Following this, I pursued my graduate training at the University of California at San Diego, Scripps Institute of Oceanography, and received my M.S. in 1985 and my Ph.D. in 1991. I came to the University of

Hawaii in February of 1992 as an assistant researcher and became an assistant professor in January of 1995.

"Essentially, I was hired at the University of Hawaii right out of graduate school (although I spent about nine months doing postdoctorate work at Scripps Institute of Oceanography before actually starting my job). I was hired in a competitive search, postdoctorate position known as the SOEST Young Investigator. This position is better than a simple postdoctorate in that it is actually a research faculty position (at the assistant level) that allows one to write grant proposals to federal funding agencies and to work independent of a supervisor. SOEST offers one or two of these positions a year, with applicants being chosen from a variety of disciplines (earth sciences, oceanography, marine biology, atmospheric sciences, and ocean engineering). Other universities offer these sorts of institutional postdoctorate positions with varying levels of support and duration.

"Once at the University of Hawaii, I entered into an agreement with our school's dean and other faculty to set up a state-of-the-art thermal ionization mass spectrometry facility for analyzing radioactive isotopes. This was a serious commitment for all involved, because the time frame for getting a lab of this sort funded and up and running is three to five years, longer than the two-year position I was given. However, I was given verbal agreement that, pending significant productivity on my part, my assistant researcher position could be extended beyond the original two-year period.

"At the time (1992), there were only two other facilities of this type in the country (outside of restricted-access national laboratories). Now there are probably five or so. Setting up the lab required getting federal support for the purchase of a $750,000 mass spectrometer. I funded the project with 25 percent each from the National Science Foundation Earth Sciences and Ocean Sciences Divisions and 50 percent from SOEST.

"After successfully getting the instrument funded and starting to get the laboratory set up, I was offered an assistant professor position at the University of Miami's Rosenstiel School of Marine and Atmospheric Sciences (RSMAS). At the time (spring 1994), the state of Hawaii was just entering an economic downturn, and I felt it was necessary to encourage the university into making our relationship more formal by getting a solid offer from another institution. I would have been willing to move to another locale, but preferred to continue here at UH. Following this, an assistant professor position was approved by SOEST and the UH, a national search was conducted, and I was chosen for the position. So, here I am.

"I started undergraduate school wanting to be an M.D. But during my freshman year, I became really turned on to chemistry with environmental applications. Simultaneously, I fell in love with the academician's career and lifestyle. I immediately changed my career aspirations to becoming a professor at a research university. I have nothing against private sector or government jobs and know I could find some level of fulfillment in pursuits there. However, it was clear to me then and still is today that the level of intellectual freedom that the university system in America affords makes this sort of job highly rewarding.

"I work seven days a week, between eight and twelve hours a day. Part of this may be because I am not yet tenured and part of it is because my particular brand of research requires lengthy and exacting analytical procedures in a clean room environment that makes progress slow unless you put in long hours. But part of why I work so much is simply that I enjoy it and have taken on other nonresearch and nonteaching duties as 'extras.'

"I teach one or two upper-division and/or graduate-level classroom courses per semester and presently am advising three graduate students (two Ph.D., one M.S.). I do my lab research in one- to two-month chunks where I may spend all of my nonclassroom time in the lab, in the field (both on oceangoing research vessels and on land), or in my office reducing data and interpreting results.

"Some of my fieldwork, which includes research on active volcanoes on land and on the sea floor, is 'dangerous,' and almost all of my lab work involves toxic chemicals and radioactive substances. This work isn't for everyone, but I find it rewarding because of the day-to-day challenges. The part that makes it unique and the difficult thing to pass on to students is the application of high-precision measurements requiring exacting care and uncompromising standards to natural phenomena. Although the lab and fieldwork are both necessary aspects of the research we do, the two environments are very different and require different mind-sets.

"In addition to these things, I have also worked to get our school (SOEST) and its departments, students, and faculty online to the Internet. I developed and oversee numerous websites at our school, including interactive sites providing answers to the public's questions about science and resource sites dedicated to educating laypeople and researchers about active processes at volcanoes and the latest research going on at the University of Hawaii. I use the Internet in my courses and love what it offers. Once a person relates to and accepts the way in which people make computers process and make information available, the mind is freed to cross the boundaries between the abstract and the physical. Computers are a wonderful and indispensable teaching tool.

"There are, of course, many tradeoffs with this sort of job. To enjoy the academic and intellectual freedom, friendly atmosphere, youthful environment, and flexible hours, one must be very disciplined. This can make it difficult, as you must evaluate yourself and your progress frequently and cannot rely on infrequent or nonexistent direction from a superior. You must 'sense' the expectations of one's peers and then work to satisfy them while not sacrificing one's own goals and desires. You must be self-motivated and take a very long-range perspective on success in the attainment of work-related goals.

"Additionally, today's academic scientist must deal with lack of funds at all levels. The golden age of scientific research died out in the 1980s (if not earlier). I watch my older colleagues struggling to adapt to this new environment, but since I never knew the days of seemingly unlimited research funds, I don't get as depressed as they at the difficulty of getting research funded today.

"People need to realize that jobs are very difficult to obtain, so you must always work hard at everything you do. Not only are top-notch resumes required to land one of these jobs, but hard work will be required to keep it. A university professor's life may appear to be genteel and rewarding and filled with healthy doses of wisdom and cups of cappuccino at the local coffeehouse, but it is actually rigorous on many levels."

Meet Kevin T. M. Johnson, Ph.D.

Dr. Johnson, a research geologist, is employed by both the Bishop Museum and the University of Hawaii in Honolulu, Hawaii.

"I was always interested in oceans and volcanoes, and my choice of marine geology seemed natural," explains Dr. Johnson. "Both of my parents introduced me to and encouraged me in science and academic achievement. This probably had the biggest bearing on my career—everything followed from that.

"I earned a B.S. from Penn State, an M.S. from the University of Hawaii, and my Ph.D. from MIT and Woods Hole Oceanographic Institute. Subsequently, I served as a research fellow at the University of Tokyo.

"My job is quite varied. I spend about 75 to 80 percent of my time doing basic marine geological research on projects that I have received external funding to carry out. Most of my research funding is from the National Science Foundation. Primarily, my projects deal with the formation of ocean basins and oceanic crust at mid-ocean ridges and oceanic islands. I spend months at sea each year on research expeditions collecting samples and data, then I analyze the samples and data back on land. In addition to this, I collaborate with archaeologists in studies of stone tools and secure funding from smaller agencies and contractors to carry out more specific, applied research.

"I also give public lectures on volcanoes, geology, and earth sciences and also lead field trips to Kilauea, the active volcano on the island of Hawaii. In addition, I advise museum exhibit staff on technical matters within my area of knowledge, in addition to fielding questions from the public. So I am very busy day to day and spend about sixty to seventy hours per week on the various aspects of my job. The work atmosphere at the museum and the university are quite pleasant, and I enjoy the interactions I have with my colleagues and students.

"I truly enjoy research because it allows me to pursue questions of my own choosing and to interact with interesting and intelligent people, both colleagues and students. Also, since I don't have to punch a time clock, doing research gives me a lot of flexibility and a relaxed schedule. The part I enjoy least is the process of research proposal writing because it takes a considerable amount of time to write a good proposal and the competition for funds is very keen.

"My advice to other scientific types is to be very studious in school and in life in general. Enjoy the world around you and be inquisitive about the natural phenomena you observe every day. Ask questions and think about possible answers."

Meet Glen D. Lawrence, Ph.D.

Dr. Lawrence, professor of chemistry, has been affiliated with Long Island University since 1985. He received his B.S. in chemistry from Pratt Institute in Brooklyn, New York; his M.A. in chemistry from SUNY at Plattsburgh, New York; and his Ph.D. in biochemistry from Utah State University in Logan. He served as a science advisor for the U.S. Food and Drug Administration, New York Regional Laboratory, from 1988 to 1992, advising analytical chemists in research projects related to drug chemistry.

"I grew up on a farm in rural New York State and always had a curiosity about how living organisms functioned," says Dr. Lawrence. "However, I had few role models who were scientists in my community (in fact none that I can think of) and a very poor guidance counselor in high school, so I had little idea what direction I wanted to take after completing high school. I did well in science and math in school and decided to pursue a career in chemistry. As I began studying chemistry, I realized that my fascination was with biochemistry, so I enrolled in a master's degree program in a chemistry department, with a biochemist as my research advisor. This mentor was recommended by one of my high school friends who had gone to that college as an undergraduate. After completing my master's degree, I had a taste of the academic research life and knew that I wanted to pursue that option. I applied to graduate school in Utah at the suggestion of one of the professors where I had received my master's degree and went there to study for my doctorate in biochemistry.

"After completing my Ph.D., I applied for a research fellowship to study model systems for photosynthesis, with the support of a National Science Foundation energy-related postdoctoral fellowship. I was always conservation minded and wanted to do studies on the development of materials that could be used to convert solar energy into useful chemical energy. This specific project was aimed at developing materials that would utilize light to catalyze the splitting of water into hydrogen and oxygen, which could later be used as fuels. After studying this problem for a year in West Germany (1976–1977), I came to the realization that it was a difficult task to accomplish (mimicking nature generally is not easy to accomplish in the chemistry laboratory). I spent several years pursuing research at several different laboratories (University of California at Riverside, Mt. Sinai, and Columbia University) and found these research opportunities to be extremely valuable to me in broadening my knowledge of science in general, and biochemistry, pharmacology, physiology, and toxicology in particular.

"I started at LIU in 1985, while a research fellow in the Institute of Human Nutrition at Columbia University. Funding for my research project was ending, and, although I was coauthor of another funded research grant, there had been an administrative error that made me ineligible for financial support from that grant for another year. I therefore actively pursued a teaching position, which was my ultimate career goal. Although I was planning to hold out for a faculty position at a 'research' institution, the master's degree program at LIU, Brooklyn Campus, provided ample opportunity for research, along with interesting possibilities for teaching advanced courses in special areas, such as neurochemistry and advanced analytical techniques for biomedical analysis.

"As a professor of chemistry in a department that offers a master's degree, I am responsible for teaching about nine hours of courses per week during a typical academic year. I teach a wide range of college courses, including any of the following during any given academic year: introductory chemistry for nonscience (liberal arts) majors (three hours of lecture and two hours of lab per week); chemistry for the health sciences (three hours of lecture and two and a half hours of lab per week); biochemistry to chemistry and molecular biology majors (three hours of lecture and three hours of lab per week); and graduate courses in analytical chemistry, biochemistry, and neurochemistry (each three hours of lecture per week). Occasionally I offer an elective course for honors students (the one last fall was titled Drugs in Our Culture). Of course I don't teach all of these courses in any given year, since it adds up to much more than nine hours per week.

"In addition to teaching, I usually advise undergraduate and graduate students in research projects This past spring I had two undergraduate students working with me on two separate projects. One student was analyzing naltrexone, a morphinelike drug that was being used in a study with hypertensive, stroke-prone rats. The animal study was performed by a colleague in the School of Pharmacy at LIU. Our job in the chemistry department was to measure the drug taken from blood samples from these rats. The amount of blood you can get from a rat is very small (about 0.5 ml), so our procedure had to be suitable for measuring tiny amounts of this potent drug in very small amounts. We were successful in developing the method, after much time was spent trying to fine-tune the analytical instrument needed to make these measurements.

"The other project was a study of the effect of combining vitamin C with aspartame (the artificial sweetener known as Nutrasweet) and measuring the products that result from combining these two food additives. We were interested to see if there are any products that could be potentially harmful to our health. Again, this requires the analysis of trace amounts of substances in a complex mixture of things.

"The lab that my students and I work in is very small and cramped (only about seven feet by fifteen feet, including a sink, a hood, a cabinet for glassware, and bench space for pH meter, stirrers for mixing solutions, and some small analytical instruments). Some of the instruments we use are in another large room that contains only special analytical instruments.

"Although the work is not dangerous, we must take the proper precautions when performing some experiments. The materials we work with are usually not explosive in nature, nor are most of them very toxic. However, we must be aware of the things that are toxic or explosive and handle them in a way that is not going to result in a perilous situation.

"Some years ago, I worked as a science advisor for the Food and Drug Administration. That job required that I go to the

FDA labs one day a week and discuss research projects with the analytical chemists there. Their jobs primarily involved analyzing the drugs being sold by pharmaceutical companies. The FDA must use well-established methods for drug analysis, which have undergone extensive testing in both the FDA labs as well as the pharmaceutical manufacturers' labs. Some of these methods rely on procedures that may be many years old, but newer methods could save much time without sacrificing accuracy. However, any new method must be tested before it can become an established method in their protocol. My job was to work with the chemists there to try to streamline the methods used to accomplish efficient and accurate drug analysis.

"One example was a method for analyzing the drugs in nerve gas antidotes for the U.S. Department of Defense. When the Persian Gulf War broke out, nerve gas antidotes had to be removed from storage and tested quickly to make sure they were suitable for use, since much of the stockpile had passed the expiration date. The existing method required approximately forty-five minutes per sample for testing. I tried a different method that I thought would work, and it resulted in decreasing the analysis time to about ten minutes. This isn't a great deal for a few samples, but when there were hundreds of lots of drug samples that had to be analyzed, this decrease in time would mean a savings of weeks or months in analysis time. However, the new method had to be thoroughly tested before it could be implemented. It turned out to be very suitable, not only for military samples but for a wide variety of dosage forms, including eye drops and some other medications.

"As a professor, I also serve on various committees around the campus. Though these committees vary from year to year, all take up a substantial amount of time. The committee work may include the evaluation of junior faculty members for promotion and tenure, discussion of new courses and curricula that are being proposed for the university, review of existing courses and programs, the regular reevaluation of the campus for accreditation, or attention to the day-to-day running of the university.

"In addition, I am often asked to review a master's degree candidate's thesis to determine whether the student meets our approval to obtain a degree. If I am the student's advisor, it may require sitting down with the candidate, advising him or her how to go about writing a master's thesis, and reading the thesis over many times to make all the necessary corrections before it is submitted to the student's committee. This all occurs after guiding the student through a research project that usually lasts about a year. Although the student doesn't work on the project full-time, he or she may put in ten to twenty hours per week doing the research in the lab. This requires developing methods for analyzing certain chemicals that may be of interest to us, collecting a wealth of data to support a hypothesis, and analyzing that data to see if it does support the hypothesis, then finally deciding how to present the data so it will be understandable to others who may be interested.

"Whether in the classroom or the laboratory, teaching can be very exciting. Other times it can be extremely frustrating. Sometimes students show a genuine interest in the material; other times I get a whole classroom of students who just don't want to be there (but it is a requirement for them to graduate). Many come into the class dreading it initially but find after a while that we are covering things that can be quite interesting, such as the greenhouse effect, global warming, air and water pollution, destruction of the ozone layer, and guidelines about how to keep your body healthy. By the time the students get finished, some of them realize that it was a worthwhile college experience.

"Probably the most rewarding aspect of my job is realized when a student decides to do a special project, either in the form of research in the lab or a library research project, and that student begins to comprehend the complexities of science, especially the life sciences. If I feel that I could instill in another individual the desire to pursue a career in science or just to understand more about how the world works on the molecular level, then I feel I have accomplished my goal. Even if only a handful of my students realize this in my lifetime, I will have passed something on to the next generation.

"I was never a specialist, and I don't feel it is necessary to be a specialist to be successful in science, although specialization is the norm. It's important to take advantage of every opportunity to learn, however, whether it is from what seems to be a failure or what seems to be a success. And the most important thing in life is to be satisfied (or happy) with what you are doing. Some people feel it is necessary to work at a job to make money, so you can enjoy yourself in the relatively few hours you may have to yourself. But if you enjoy your work, you will not have to spend so much of your money trying to get away from your work."

Meet Charles L. Dumoulin, Ph.D.

Dr. Dumoulin, a research scientist, serves as a physicist in the field of medicine. He has been on staff at General Electric's Research and Development Center in Schenectady, New York, since 1984. In 1996, he received the center's highest honor, its Coolidge Fellowship Award, which recognizes sustained contribution to science or engineering. Dr. Dumoulin was honored for his pioneering contributions to magnetic resonance imaging (MRI). He has published eighty-three peer-reviewed papers and twenty-four chapters in books, and he has had sixty-one issued patents and currently has eleven patents pending.

"Although I was always fascinated by science as a child (and high school showed me I had a knack for science and math), my original career plan was to become a military officer," reveals Dr. Dumoulin. "When I learned that my eyesight was too poor, I changed my plans and went to Florida State University, choosing chemistry as my major. After school and during summer vacations, I worked in a television and appliance repair shop and realized that I enjoyed learning how things work (televisions, radios, washing machines, refrigerators, and so forth). I also learned that the best way to understand something was to take it apart, fix it, and put it back together. I found solving problems to be most enjoyable. As I became a researcher, I found that the most fun problems to tackle were those that required creative solutions and addressed real-life problems. I also found that, unlike many fields, science generally dealt with questions that have objective and provable answers.

"Subsequently, I earned a Ph.D. from Florida State University in analytical chemistry in 1981. After I received my Ph.D., I moved with my thesis professor to Syracuse University, where I became a nontenure-track assistant professor. For three years I helped run a lab, did some research, and was cofounder of a small company. I came to realize, however, that this environment was not allowing me to develop as a researcher.

"I then moved to GE's Research and Development Center, where I changed my focus from nuclear magnetic resonance spectroscopy for chemistry to the related topic of magnetic resonance (MR) for medical applications.

"For the last thirteen years I have been working as a physicist in the field of medicine. I have worked primarily to develop new ways to perform diagnostic and interventional procedures with magnetic resonance imaging (MRI) scanners. Major projects that I have led or been a part of include MR spectroscopy, MR angiography (use of radio frequency signals to follow devices in real time), MR measurements of kidney function, MR tracking of interventional devices in real time, cardiac MR imaging, and use of MR to increase basic understanding of flow physiology in blood vessels.

"Although I'm paid to work forty hours per week, I typically work eight to nine hours per day and frequently a few hours during the weekend. Even when I'm not working, I often find myself thinking about problems at work. Some of my most productive moments occur while trying to sleep and driving to or from work.

"As a scientist working in industry, my job is somewhat different than that of an academic scientist working in a university. For example, I have to justify my work as having some relevance to my company. Consequently, most of what I do can be called 'applied science' rather than 'basic science.'

"The work atmosphere here is relatively relaxed, yet there is always a certain intensity of purpose. I am surrounded by extremely capable colleagues who have been trained in a number of different scientific disciplines (such as computer science, physical chemistry, physics, astrophysics, medicine, electrical engineering). We tend to work in ad hoc teams, and conflicts are rare. Every Friday we meet to discuss topics as diverse as life in the universe, politics, or even Dilbert.

"A nice aspect of my job is that every day brings unique challenges and tasks. A typical day begins with the reading and answering of E-mail. I interact with many people in Europe and Japan, and we have found that E-mail is the best way to communicate. One or two days each week I sign up to use the MRI scanner in our building. I spend those days testing new ideas and performing experiments. When I'm not in the lab, I can usually be found at my desk writing (E-mail, memos, papers, and so on) or in meetings with my colleagues.

"My job frequently requires me to travel. My trips often take me to conferences, where I speak about my work and listen to other scientists speak about theirs. I find that these talks are often a great source of inspiration. Other trips take me to different research hospitals around the world where I work with doctors to develop and evaluate new ways of using MRI scanners.

"To me the best part of this career is the intellectual challenge of finding creative solutions to problems, the exposure to new ideas within and beyond my profession, and working on medical diagnostic methods that have direct relevance to patients. I also enjoy the latitude I have to define my own research agenda (although I wish I had more), working with some of the best scientists and engineers in the world, and the opportunity to talk to students of all ages about science and technology.

"The more negative aspects of this career include the fact that things get in the way of productivity and the difficulty of securing funding for projects and patent protection for all of my inventions. Also, there is a lack of tenure in the industry, compensation for scientists is not commensurate with their contributions to society, and there is a lack of wide-ranging opportunities for people in my specialty.

"I would recommend to all prospective scientists that you remain as broad as possible. Scientific success often occurs by the synergistic combination of two or more existing ideas from different disciplines.

"It's important to stay focused on completing projects. But somehow you must concentrate on each project at every stage of its being. And usually a project is not considered complete until a publication (for example, memo, paper, patent application) is submitted.

"It is always in your best interests to use the golden rule when dealing with everyone. Be particularly sensitive to the issue of sharing credit with your coworkers. Virtually all discoveries are accomplished as a result of the efforts of many—be sure everyone gets their just portion of the rewards!"

Meet Eric S. Posmentier, Ph.D.

Dr. Posmentier serves as professor of physics and mathematics at the Brooklyn Campus of Long Island University, New York. He earned a B.S. from the City College of New York in 1964 (physics) and a Ph.D. from Columbia University in 1968 (geophysics). At a time when global warming was still viewed with skepticism by many scientists, Posmentier and his colleagues at Columbia University, using data from the tropical Pacific Ocean, published evidence that global warming had begun. Posmentier is currently working with scientists at the Harvard/Smithsonian

Astrophysical Observatory to study variations of the brightness of the sun.

"Ever since elementary school, I have been fascinated by nature and curious about explanations of natural phenomena," says Dr. Posmentier. "I was drawn to any kind of scientific activity I had the opportunity to pursue, such as collecting rocks, dissecting a dead bird, or experimenting with a chemistry set 'inherited' from an older cousin. By high school, I knew that I wanted a career in the physical sciences or mathematics. In college, I discovered that geophysical sciences (physics of the atmosphere, oceans, and solid earth) held the greatest attraction for me. That is what I have concentrated on ever since, until I recently added quantum mechanics to my active research.

"The development of my interests is largely the gift of teachers and professors who gave me confidence in myself and who shared their excitement of discovering knowledge, skills, and concepts. Two particularly formative experiences stand out in my memory. One was a Bronx High School of Science sophomore course devoted to individual biology research projects. In that course, I learned how challenging it is to design an original experiment and how rewarding it is to succeed. The other experience was the opportunity to work part-time (while still in college) with graduate students and Ph.D.s in a research laboratory at Columbia University. There I discovered how satisfying it can be to apply the concepts and skills I was still in the process of acquiring in my classes to unsolved problems, making some progress, and uncovering still new questions.

"While in college, I recognized that geophysics combined several of my greatest passions: studying the exciting frontiers of understanding our planet, applying the fascinating disciplines of physics and mathematics, and spending time in the outdoors observing. I am especially attracted to problems that cross specializations within which many scientists confine themselves: for example, the physics of global warming and the economics of energy use, or ocean currents and the fishing industry, or seismic detection of earthquakes and explosions and the politics of disarmament. As a professor, I also enjoy transmitting my knowledge of and excitement for science to the next generation.

"On most days, I am in my office for up to eleven hours. I spend roughly half my time preparing classes, lecturing, meeting with students, writing, grading exams, and meeting with other professors to discuss academic matters. The other half of my time is spent reading and doing my own research. Occasionally my research has taken me to mountains to observe the air and clouds, or rocks and forests, or by boat or scuba to rivers, lakes, bays, and the ocean to observe the water and its movement. Most of my research time, however, is spent at my desk or computer. I tend to be involved in several things at once, so my typical day is busy and hectic, but there are always times when I can change the pace by having informal discussions with colleagues about my work or theirs. The ideas that come out of these informal discussions are frequently as important, in their own way, as the results of the long, disciplined hours spent alone writing, deriving mathematics, or computing. When I am deeply engrossed in a research problem it often 'comes home' with me, and I find myself working on it in the evenings and weekends, as well.

"I experience the very best part of this work at the moment a new concept is discovered and the instant my students catch on to a concept I am teaching. Least favorite is grading, grading, grading.

"I would advise that you emphasize the fundamental sciences and mathematics in your courses. You should study interdisciplinary applications, such as environmental science or marine science only in addition to—never instead of—physics, chemistry, biology, and mathematics. The latter are the foundation upon which all the rest will have to stand. Find a teacher or professor who is willing to guide you in formulating and working on an individual research problem for a week, a year, or a lifetime."

For More Information

General information on career opportunities and earnings for chemists is available from:

American Chemical Society
Education Division
1155 Sixteenth Street NW
Washington, DC 20036

For general information on opportunities in physics, write to:

American Institute of Physics
Career Planning and Placement
One Physics Ellipse
College Park, MD 20740
Homepage: http://www.aip.org

The American Physical Society
Education Department
One Physics Ellipse
College Park, MD 20740
Homepage: http://www.aps.org

For a pamphlet on careers in astronomy, send your request to:

American Astronomical Society
Education Office
Adler Planetarium and Astronomy Museum
1300 South Lake Shore Drive
Chicago, IL 60605
Homepage: http://www.aas.org

Information on opportunities for geologists is available from:

American Geological Institute
4220 King Street
Alexandria, VA 22302
Homepage: http://www.agiweb.org

Geological Society of America
P.O. Box 9140
3300 Penrose Place
Boulder, CO 80301
Homepage: http://www.geosociety.org

American Association of Petroleum Geologists
Communications Department
P.O. Box 979
Tulsa, OK 74101

Information on training and career opportunities for geophysicists is available from:

American Geophysical Union
2000 Florida Avenue NW
Washington, DC 20009

A list of education and training programs in oceanography and related fields is available from:

Marine Technology Society
1828 L Street NW, Suite 906
Washington, DC 20036

Information on career opportunities in meteorology is available from:

American Meteorological Society
45 Beacon Street
Boston, MA 02108
Homepage: http://www.ametsoc.org/AMS

Information on acquiring a job as a chemist, physicist, astronomer, geologist, geophysicist, or meteorologist with the federal government may be obtained from the Office of Personnel Management (OPM) through a telephone-based system. Consult your telephone directory under U.S. Government for a local number, or visit the website at http://www.usajobs.opm.gov.

CHAPTER FOUR

Careers in the Agricultural Sciences

The whole of science is nothing more than a refinement of everyday thinking. ALBERT EINSTEIN

C an you think of anything more important than food? It is at the very core of our existence. Food technology incorporates the application of science to the commercial processing of foodstuffs. Foods are processed to make them more palatable or digestible; to prevent the growth of bacteria, molds, yeasts, and other microorganisms; or to preserve them from spoiling—a process caused by the action of enzymes within the food that changes its chemical composition, resulting in changes in flavor, odor, color, and texture. For instance, preservation enables foods that are seasonally produced to be available all year. Such is the work of agricultural scientists.

Agricultural Scientists

The work of agricultural scientists plays an important part in maintaining and increasing the nation's agricultural productivity. Agricultural scientists study farm crops and animals and develop ways of improving their quantity and quality. They look for ways to improve crop yield and quality with less labor, avenues to control pests and weeds more safely and effectively, and techniques to conserve soil and water. They research methods of converting raw agricultural commodities into attractive and healthy food products for consumers.

Agricultural science is closely related to biological science. Scientists in this field use the principles of biology, chemistry, and other sciences to solve problems in agriculture. They often work with biological scientists on basic biological research, or they may concentrate on applying the technological advances to agriculture.

Many agricultural scientists work in basic or applied research and development. Others manage or administer research and development programs or manage marketing or production operations in companies that produce food products or agricultural chemicals, supplies, and machinery. Some agricultural scientists are consultants to business firms, private clients, or government agencies.

The nature of the work performed will vary according to the agricultural scientist's area of specialization.

Food Science

Food scientists or food technologists are usually employed in the food processing industry, at universities, or by the gederal government. They help meet consumer demand for food products that are healthful, safe, palatable, and convenient. To do this, they use their knowledge of chemistry, microbiology, and other sciences to develop new or better ways of preserving, processing, packaging, storing, and delivering foods.

Some food scientists engage in basic research, working on projects involving the discovery of new food sources; the analysis of food content to determine levels of vitamins, fat, sugar, or protein; or the search for potential substitutes for harmful or undesirable food additives, such as nitrites. Many food technologists work in product development. Others enforce government regulations, inspecting food processing areas and ensuring that sanitation, safety, quality, and waste management standards are met.

Plant Science

Plant science includes the disciplines of agronomy, crop science, entomology, and plant breeding, among others. Scientists in these areas study plants and their growth in soils, helping producers of food, feed, and fiber crops to continue to feed a growing population while conserving natural resources and maintaining the environment. Agronomists and crop scientists not only help increase productivity but also study ways to improve the nutritional value of crops and the quality of seed. Some crop scientists study the breeding, physiology, and management of crops and use genetic engineering to develop crops resistant to pests and drought.

Soil Science

Soil scientists explore the chemical, physical, biological, and mineralogical composition of soils as they relate to plant or crop growth. They study the responses of various soil types to fertilizers, tillage practices, and crop rotation. Many soil scientists who work for the federal government conduct soil surveys, classifying and mapping soils. They provide information and recommendations to farmers and other landowners regarding the best use of land and how to avoid or correct problems such as erosion. They may also consult with engineers and other technical personnel working on construction projects about the effects of, and solutions to, soil problems. Since soil science is closely related to environmental science, people trained in soil science also apply their knowledge to ensure environmental quality and effective land use.

Animal Science

Animal scientists develop better, more efficient ways of producing and processing meat, poultry, eggs, and milk. Dairy scientists, poultry scientists, animal breeders, and other related scientists study the genetics, nutrition, reproduction, growth, and development of domestic farm animals. Some animal scientists inspect and grade livestock—or other food products—purchase livestock, or work in technical sales or marketing. As extension agents or consultants, animal scientists advise agricultural producers on how to upgrade animal housing facilities properly, lower mortality rates, or increase production of animal products, such as milk or eggs. Entomologists, who also fall under the animal science area, may talk to local farmers about insect problems in growing corn and other crops.

Education and Training for Agricultural Scientists

Training requirements for agricultural scientists depend on the specialty and the type of work they perform. A bachelor's degree in agricultural science is sufficient for some jobs in applied research or in assisting in basic research, but a master's or doctoral degree is required for basic research. A doctoral degree in agricultural science is usually needed to qualify for college teaching and for advancement to administrative research positions. Degrees in related sciences, such as biology, chemistry, or physics, or in related engineering specialties also may qualify persons for some agricultural science jobs.

All states have a land-grant college that offers agricultural science degrees. Many other colleges and universities also offer agricultural science degrees or some agricultural science courses, although not every school offers all specialties.

A typical undergraduate agricultural science curriculum includes communications, economics, business, and physical and life sciences courses, in addition to a wide variety of technical agricultural science courses. For prospective animal scientists,

these agricultural courses might include animal breeding, repro-
ductive physiology, nutrition, and meats and muscle biology. Students preparing to become food scientists take courses such as
food chemistry, food analysis, food microbiology, and food processing operations. Those preparing to be crop or soil scientists
take courses in plant pathology, soil chemistry, entomology, plant
physiology, and biochemistry, among others. Advanced degree
programs include classroom and fieldwork, laboratory research,
and a thesis based on independent research.

Agricultural scientists should be able to work independently or
as part of a team and be able to communicate clearly and concisely, both orally and in writing. Most agricultural scientists also
need an understanding of basic business principles.

Agricultural scientists who have advanced degrees usually
begin in research or teaching. With experience, they could
advance to supervising research programs or managing other
agriculture-related activities.

Job Outlook for Agricultural Scientists

Employment of agricultural scientists is expected to grow about
as fast as the average for all occupations through the year 2006.
The need to replace agricultural scientists who retire or otherwise leave the occupation permanently will account for many of
the job openings.

Although the number of degrees awarded in agricultural
science programs has been steady or even declined since the
1980s, new entrants, even those with advanced degrees, may still
face competition for jobs as agricultural scientists. Animal and
plant scientists with a background in molecular biology, microbiology, genetics, or biotechnology; soil scientists with an interest
in the environment; and food technologists may find the best
opportunities.

Generally speaking, those with advanced degrees will be in the best position to secure jobs as agricultural scientists. However, competition for teaching positions in colleges or universities and for some basic research jobs may be keen, even for doctoral holders, since federal and state budget cuts may limit funding for these positions through the year 2006.

Bachelor's degree holders can work in some applied research and product development positions, but usually only in certain subfields, such as food science and technology. The federal government hires bachelor's degree holders to work as soil scientists. Despite the more limited job opportunities for those with only bachelor's degrees, a bachelor's degree in agricultural science is useful for managerial jobs in businesses that deal with ranchers and farmers, such as feed, fertilizer, seed, and farm equipment manufacturers; retailers or wholesalers; and farm credit institutions. Four-year degrees may also help persons seeking occupations such as cooperative extension service agents, farmers or farm or ranch managers, agricultural products inspectors, technicians, landscape architects, or purchasing or sales agents for agricultural commodities or farm supplies.

Salaries for Agricultural Scientists

According to the National Association of Colleges and Employers, beginning salary offers in 1997 for graduates with bachelor's degrees in animal science averaged about $24,900 a year, and for graduates in plant science, $24,000.

According to a salary survey performed by the Institute of Food Technology, the median salary for full-time food scientists or technologists is about $55,000.

Average federal salaries for employees in nonsupervisory, supervisory, and managerial positions in agricultural science specialties in 1997 were as follows: animal science, $65,500; agronomy, $52,000; soil science, $49,400; horticulture, $50,400; entomology, $62,200.

Parade of Professionals

Meet Carl I. Evensen, Ph.D.

Dr. Evensen serves as assistant extension specialist for natural resource management and environmental quality in the Department of Agronomy and Soil Science at the University of Hawaii.

"All my life, I have enjoyed gardening and growing crops, so the decision to go into agriculture as a profession seemed very natural to me," Dr. Evensen says. "I also like working with other people and have found that I truly enjoy agricultural extension work, since it combines these interests and inclinations.

"After I earned my bachelor's degree in Biology from Whitman College in Walla Walla, Washington, I was still very unsure of what profession to choose. So I decided that to give myself some time to think and to try to 'give something back,' I would join the Peace Corps. Thus, I spent two years in Kenya working as a horticultural extensionist in an isolated part of the Coast Province called the Taita Hills. This was a wonderful, life-changing experience that not only convinced me that I wanted to work in agriculture but also pointed out the gaps in my knowledge.

"I then determined that I would go back to school to study agriculture and decided on the strong tropical agriculture program at the University of Hawaii. My master's program was spent studying agroforestry in Hawaii, while my doctoral research was performed in Indonesia, working on a soil management project. These studies gave me a strong background in soil fertility and crop nutrition, which I continue to use in my current job. Also these overseas work experiences really broadened my perspective and helped me tremendously in understanding the needs of foreign graduate students. My subsequent job as an agronomist (1989–1993) at the Hawaii Sugar Planter's Association (HSPA) was very valuable in giving me experience with large-scale, plantation agriculture, as a contrast to my previous work with small-scale, subsistence farmers. Also at HSPA, I began to work with soil and water conservation issues and problems.

"I feel this type of job is very rewarding but also overwhelming and all consuming. It is important to be organized and frequently reprioritize the multiple and changing activities so that the really critical things get done in a timely manner. However, it is also very important to avoid becoming consumed by the job. Your must make time for yourself and your family because there is a danger of becoming burned out."

Meet Michael Moore, Ph.D.

Dr. Moore, a taxonomist, serves as the curator of the Plant Department at the University of Georgia.

"As an undergraduate at the University of Georgia, I was already interested in this field," says Dr. Moore. "So I stayed on as a graduate student and earned my master's degree in 1985 and my doctorate in 1989. I was lucky enough to get a job at the university even before I finished school. I've been the curator of the herbarium (plant museum) in the Plant Department of the University of Georgia for three years.

"The herbarium at the University of Georgia is the largest in the state of Georgia. We have just over two hundred thousand mounted specimens. My responsibilities as curator are to make sure that the collection is maintained and curated in a proper manner. I also have research projects that take me out into the field. This past year, for instance, I was out in the field every other week between March and October. I enjoy the fact that I work both inside and out-of-doors.

"We curators also have a responsibility to respond to questions from the public. Additionally, we exchange specimens with other herbaria, loan plants, and handle plant identifications as they come in. Over the years I have also taught some classes at the university. Taxonomists may be called upon to do many things.

"It's important to realize that a master's degree is usually a requirement and a doctorate is preferred for those who wish to embark upon this career. If you wish to focus on academia, you can do research as well as teach. Then you would want a heavy background in molecular biology and similar course work. If you want to be more of a field botanist—that is, someone who does more or less what I do in herbaria—or work with a private company protecting endangered species, you would want to have more ornamental horticulture training.

"Most major universities have herbaria. The number of curators they have will depend on how many specimens they house. For example, in very large herbaria there will be individual curators who will be responsible for certain species of categories of plants.

"There are a number of hot topics that require the services of professionals in this field: conservation of the rain forest and environmental issues for example. In the future, I think there will still be jobs for those who have a good basic background in taxonomy and are able to do basic field research."

Meet Art Davis, Ph.D.

Dr. Davis, a cereal chemist, is the director of scientific services at the American Association of Cereal Chemists, where he has served for the past two years.

"I obtained my bachelor's degree from Oregon State University and spent two years in the Peace Corps," says Dr. Davis. "Then I went on to graduate school at Kansas State University, where I earned a master's degree and a doctorate in cereal chemistry. I always knew I was headed into biology and the sciences.

"After working for the Pillsbury Company in its research and development department, I assumed a position heading a research group for the American Institute of Baking for about two and a half years. Following that, I served on the faculty of Kansas State University for nine years. Subsequent positions included quality assurance manager for General Foods Bakeries and three years as the director of technical services for the Green Giant Fresh Vegetables Group.

"Here at the American Association of Cereal Chemists, the main thing we do is offer about thirty short courses and other continuing education programs. Whenever there's a need to provide basic information in food science, we fill that void. For instance, there's been a tremendous growth in the use of frozen foods in this country in the last six or seven years, and a lot of (particularly smaller) companies are interested in getting into that field. Since there was no training available, we went out and found some people who were knowledgeable about this topic and put together a two-day course that provides the basics for those who need this information.

"Other courses we offer include water activity, wet milling sensory analysis, food technology, batter and breading technology, chemical leavening, breakfast cereal technology, chemistry technology, and principles of cereal science. Individuals often come to us with biology, microbiology, or engineering backgrounds but no experience with food. So for individuals both overseas and here in the states, our courses provide the information needed.

"Another service we provide is an international check sample service. Monthly, bimonthly, or quarterly, samples are sent to participating laboratories. Specific analysis is performed and the results are sent to us. We then compile all of the results and provide a report that reveals the status of perhaps a hundred laboratories. This gives the labs some idea of whether or not they are in line with other labs and how accurate their findings are. In fact, this year we're starting to do some proficiency certification. If you send all of the samples in for a year and your results are in line with the other labs, we'll issue you a certificate verifying that fact.

"Because there's a critical size that must be reached before it's feasible to establish your own research and development group, smaller companies tend to depend on their suppliers to do their research and development for them. For instance, my experience at the General Foods Bakeries taught me that you can mix doughnut batter—starting with flour, sugar, salt, and so forth—without a problem. However, because of some of the peculiarities of putting doughnut mixes together, it's a lot more efficient to buy a mix from a company that makes doughnut mixes. If you've got a problem with it, you can ask them to solve it, or it you want something a little bit different, you can ask them to create that for you. Flavor houses, mix suppliers, and fats and oils suppliers have their own research and development divisions, as do some of the bakers and mills. These are the people who can get you the properties you want. Thus they'll go into their labs and massage the molecules until they come up with what you are looking for.

"For those interested in getting into food science, I would highly recommend Kansas State University's Department of Grain Science and Industry. They've got three curricula there: milling, baking, and seed plants (which has to do with building animal feeds). The undergraduate program, which includes serious chemistry, physics, and a little bit of engineering, is so excellent that every student who graduates from there has at least a couple of job offers. There is also a graduate program, and they never have any trouble placing those people either.

"Minnesota has a small but growing program in the cereals area through their food science department. Iowa State and Texas A&M do some good work. It's not labeled food science—I think it's called crop and food science. At the graduate level, Kansas State and North Dakota State University have good graduate programs, and Texas A&M has a graduate group that works in cereals, as does Iowa State. Just drop a line to those universities and see if their programs are of interest to you.

"If you are planning on doing research at a university, I'd recommend that you get a Ph.D. However, industry doesn't get terribly hung up on degrees. I know a number of good researchers with master's degrees who have gone on and done quite well. I even know of a few with bachelor's degrees who have distinguished themselves. If you are an able researcher, there are opportunities out there for you."

Meet Brent Steven Sipes, Ph.D.

Dr. Sipes is employed by the University of Hawaii's Department of Plant Pathology in Honolulu in the capacity of assistant plant pathologist. He came to the university as a junior researcher in 1991 to evaluate pineapple for resistance or tolerance to a plant parasite.

"I very much enjoy the outdoors and plants," says Dr. Sipes. "As a child, my next-door neighbor, a grandmotherly teacher, encouraged me to garden. This interest in plants and their biology, systematics, and cultivation has followed me ever since.

"Majoring in plant pathology, I received my B.S. degree from Purdue University in West Lafayette, Indiana, in 1983. With the same specialty, I earned my M.S. and Ph.D. from North Carolina State University in Raleigh in 1987 and 1991, respectively.

"Growing up in the sixties and seventies, I was also very conscientious of environmental stewardship. This activism motivated me to help in the proper use of pesticides, which are necessary to avoid problems that seem to plague agricultural production. Becoming a plant pathologist, someone who studies plant diseases and their control, was a natural outgrowth of all this.

"My first job was in a commercial greenhouse in Louisville, Kentucky. We grew roses, which were shipped all over the Midwest, regularly treating all of the plants with chemicals to ensure acceptable quality and maintain production. This was an enjoy-able job but physically exhausting. It taught me that I didn't want to be a common laborer the rest of my life.

"I spent three college summers working in a premier institute, the Morton Arboretum, located in a suburb of Chicago. I was tutored by professional horticulturists who cared about plants and their well-being. These people instilled within me the desire to perform quality work that would ensure that future genera-tions would enjoy the plants in the collections of the arboretum. I learned much about plant classification—what made a rose a rose and a maple a maple (rather than an oak).

"I did well in college and knew before graduation that I would pursue an advanced degree. Graduate school agreed with me. I enjoyed the thrill of collecting and analyzing data from experi-ments and of formulating and asking questions. I enjoyed con-ducting research.

"Today, in my capacity as assistant professor, my days can vary greatly. Some are spent indoors moving from one committee meeting to the next. Others are spent at my desk analyzing and preparing data for presentations. Perhaps the best ones are those when I am outside in the field collecting samples, setting up a test, or treating an experiment. Sometimes I am asked to travel to experiments on neighboring islands, and I attend scientific meetings all over the world.

"I am at liberty to structure my day as I see fit. I like to start early while the day is cool (around 7 A.M.) and finish before it gets really hot (by about 4 P.M), even if I am working inside all day. Because 60 percent of my work involves field experiments, much of its completion depends upon the weather. Rain can real-ly ruin our best plans. Consequently, sometimes the work is very slow and easy, whereas other times everything needs to be done and there is hardly any time to breathe. In total, I work about forty-eight to fifty hours per week, but since I enjoy my job, I usu-ally don't keep track of the hours.

"My job requires me to work with many different types of people—from senior professors and administrators to technical staff who assist me in my research to students. Each group is different and the challenge is to work well with everyone.

"The people in my laboratory are much like a family. Although we may not always share the same opinions, we get along well together.

"What I like most about my work is the ability to pose questions and contemplate how to answer them. I like to analyze data in order to answer those questions. And I am honored by the respect my work affords me in the community.

"If you are interested and excited by this career, then commit yourself to it. The most important aspect to living is to enjoy your livelihood. Do not work to live on the weekends."

For More Information

General information on careers in agricultural science is available from:

American Society of Agronomy
Crop Science Society of America
Soil Science Society of America
677 South Segoe Road
Madison, WI 53711

Food and Agricultural Careers for Tomorrow
Purdue University
1140 Agricultural Administration Building
West Lafayette, IN 47907

For information on career opportunities in food technology, write to:

Institute of Food Technologists
Suite 300, 221 North LaSalle Street
Chicago, IL 60601

For information on careers in entomology, contact:

Entomological Society of America
Attn: Public Relations Coordinator
9301 Annapolis Road
Lanham, MD 20706

Information on acquiring a job as an agricultural scientist with
the federal government may be obtained from the Office of Personnel Management through a telephone-based system. Consult
your telephone directory under U.S. Government for a local
number or visit the website at http://www.usajobs.opm.gov.

CHAPTER FIVE

Careers in Engineering

The outcome of any serious research can only be to make two questions grow where one question grew before. THORSTEIN VEBLEN

H istoric engineering feats during the twentieth century include the Golden Gate Bridge in 1937, television in 1931, the Apollo moon landing in 1969, the Panama Canal in 1914, the artificial heart in 1967, nuclear power in the 1950s, fiber-optic communications in 1977, the trans-Alaska pipeline in 1977, the Empire State Building in 1931, the procedure known as the cat scan in the1970s, the microprocessor in 1958, jumbo jets in 1969, lasers in 1956, computer-aided design in the 1970s, and the electron microscope in 1931. All of these incredible advances were the result of intense effort on the part of countless engineers who endeavored to develop new and improved products, technological advances, and healthier and more prosperous ways to live.

If this is a career path that appeals to you, read on to learn about what it's like to be an engineer.

Engineers

Engineers apply the theories and principles of science and mathematics to the economical solution of practical technical problems. Usually their work is the link between a scientific discovery and its commercial application.

It is the responsibility of engineers to create machinery, products, systems, and processes for efficient and economical performance. They design industrial machinery and equipment for manufacturing defense-related goods and weapons systems for the armed forces in addition to designing, planning, and supervising the construction of buildings, highways, and rapid transit systems. They also design and develop systems for control and automation of manufacturing, business, and management.

Engineers consider many factors in developing a new product. For example, in developing an industrial robot, they determine precisely what function it needs to perform; design and test the necessary components; fit them together in an integrated plan; and evaluate the design's overall effectiveness, cost, reliability, and safety. This process applies to products as different as chemicals, computers, gas turbines, helicopters, and toys.

In addition to design and development, many engineers work in testing, production, or maintenance. They supervise production in factories, determine the causes of breakdowns, and test manufactured products to maintain quality. They also estimate the time and cost to complete projects. Some work in engineering management or in sales, where an engineering background enables them to discuss the technical aspects of a product and assist in planning its installation or use.

Engineers use computers to simulate and test how a machine, structure, or system operates. They also use computer-aided design to produce and analyze designs. They write reports and consult with other engineers, as complex projects often require an interdisciplinary team of engineers. Supervisory engineers are responsible for major components or entire projects.

Engineering Specialties

Most engineers choose to specialize in a particular subarea. More than twenty-five major specialties are recognized by professional societies, and within the major branches are numerous subdivisions. Structural, environmental, and transportation engineering, for example, are subdivisions of civil engineering. Engineers also may specialize in one industry, such as motor vehicles, or in one field of technology, such as propulsion or guidance systems.

Aerospace Engineers

Aerospace engineers design, develop, test, and help manufacture commercial and military aircraft, missiles, and spacecraft. They develop new technologies for use in commercial aviation, defense systems, and space exploration, often specializing in areas like structural design, guidance, navigation and control, instrumentation and communication, or production methods. They also may specialize in a particular type of aerospace product, such as commercial transports, helicopters, spacecraft, or rockets. Aerospace engineers may be experts in aerodynamics, propulsion, thermodynamics, structures, celestial mechanics, acoustics, or guidance and control systems.

Chemical Engineers

Chemical engineers apply the principles of chemistry and engineering to solve problems involving the production or use of chemicals. Most chemical engineers work in the production of chemicals and chemical products.

Chemical engineers design equipment and develop processes for manufacturing chemicals, plan and test methods of manufacturing the products, and supervise production. In addition, chemical engineers work in industries other than chemical manufacturing, such as electronics or aircraft manufacturing.

Because the knowledge and duties of chemical engineers cut across many fields, they apply principles of chemistry, physics, mathematics, and mechanical and electrical engineering in their work. They frequently specialize in a particular operation, such as oxidation or polymerization. Others specialize in a particular area, such as pollution control or the production of a specific product like automotive plastics or chlorine bleach.

Civil Engineers

Civil engineers work in the oldest branch of engineering. They design and supervise the construction of roads, airports, tunnels, bridges, water-supply and sewage systems, and buildings. Major specialties within the field of civil engineering are structural, water resources, environmental, construction, transportation, and geotechnical engineering.

Many civil engineers hold supervisory or administrative positions, ranging from supervisor of a construction site to city engineer. Others may work in design, construction, research, and teaching.

Electrical and Electronics Engineers

Electrical and electronics engineers design, develop, test, and supervise the manufacture of electrical and electronic equipment. Electrical equipment includes power-generating and transmission equipment used by electric utilities; electric motors; machinery controls; and lighting and wiring in buildings, automobiles, and aircraft. Electronic equipment includes radar, computer hardware, and communications and video equipment.

The specialties of electrical and electronics engineers include several major areas, such as power generation, transmission, and distribution; communications; computer electronics; and electrical equipment manufacturing; or a subdivision of these areas, such as industrial robot control systems or aviation electronics. Electrical and electronics engineers design new products, write performance requirements, and develop maintenance schedules. They also test equipment, solve operating problems, and estimate the time and cost of engineering projects.

Industrial Engineers

Industrial engineers determine the most effective ways for an organization to use the basic factors of production—people, machines, materials, information, and energy—to make or process a product. They are the bridge between management and operations. They are more concerned with increasing productivity through the management of people, methods of business organization, and technology than are engineers in other specialties, who generally work more with products or processes.

To solve organizational, production, and related problems most efficiently, industrial engineers carefully study the product and its requirements, design manufacturing and information systems, and use mathematical analysis methods, such as operations research, to meet those requirements. They develop management control systems to aid in financial planning and cost analysis, design production planning and control systems to coordinate activities and control product quality, and design or improve systems for the physical distribution of goods and services. Industrial engineers conduct surveys to find plant locations with the best combination of raw materials, transportation, and costs. They also develop wage and salary administration systems and job evaluation programs. Many industrial engineers move into management positions because the work is closely related.

Mechanical Engineers

Mechanical engineers design tools, engines, machines, and other mechanical equipment. They also design and develop power-producing machines such as internal combustion engines, steam and gas turbines, and jet and rocket engines. They design and develop power-using machines such as refrigeration and air-conditioning equipment, robots, machine tools, materials-handling systems, and industrial production equipment.

The work of mechanical engineers varies by industry and function. Specialties include, among others, applied mechanics, design engineering, heat transfer, power-plant engineering, pressure vessels and piping, and underwater technology. Mechanical engineers design tools needed by other engineers for their work.

Mechanical engineering is the broadest engineering discipline, extending across a variety of interdependent specialties. Mechanical engineers often work in production operations, maintenance, or technical sales. Many are administrators or managers.

Metallurgical, Ceramic, and Materials Engineers

Metallurgical, ceramic, and materials engineers develop new types of metal alloys, ceramics, composites, and other materials that meet special requirements. Examples of products are graphite golf club shafts that are light but stiff, ceramic tiles on the space shuttle that protect it from burning up during reentry, and the alloy turbine blades in a jet engine.

Most metallurgical engineers work in one of the three main branches of metallurgy—extractive or chemical, physical, and mechanical or process. Extractive metallurgists are concerned with removing metals from ores and refining and alloying them to obtain useful metal. Physical metallurgists study the nature, structure, and physical properties of metals and their alloys and methods of processing them into final products. Mechanical metallurgists develop and improve metalworking processes, such as casting, forging, rolling, and drawing.

Ceramic engineers develop new ceramic materials and methods for making ceramic materials into useful products. Ceramics include all nonmetallic, inorganic materials that require high temperatures in their processing. Ceramic engineers work on products as diverse as glassware, semiconductors, automobile and aircraft engine components, fiber-optic phone lines, tile, and electric power line insulators.

Materials engineers evaluate technical requirements and material specifications to develop materials that can be used, for example, to reduce the weight, but not the strength, of an object. Materials engineers also test and evaluate materials and develop new materials, such as the composite materials now being used in "stealth" aircraft. A materials engineer uses x-ray photoelectron spectroscopy to examine the structure of a new ceramic.

Mining Engineers

Mining engineers find, extract, and prepare metals and minerals for use by manufacturing industries. They design open pit and underground mines, supervise the construction of mine shafts and tunnels in underground operations, and devise methods for transporting minerals to processing plants. Mining engineers are responsible for the safe, economical, and environmentally sound operation of mines.

Some mining engineers work with geologists and metallurgical engineers to locate and appraise new ore deposits. Others develop new mining equipment or direct mineral processing operations to separate minerals from the dirt, rock, and other materials with which they are mixed. Mining engineers frequently specialize in the mining of one mineral or metal, such as coal or gold.

With increased emphasis on protecting the environment, many mining engineers work on solving problems related to land reclamation and water and air pollution.

A mining engineer examines the plans of the current mine and those of the next phase to determine the best location for a conveyor system.

Nuclear Engineers

Nuclear engineers conduct research on nuclear energy and radiation. They design, develop, monitor, and operate nuclear power plants used to generate electricity and power navy ships. They may work on the nuclear fuel cycle; fusion energy; the production, handling, and use of nuclear fuel; and the safe disposal of waste produced by nuclear energy. Some specialize in the development of nuclear weapons; others develop industrial and medical uses for radioactive materials, such as equipment to diagnose and treat medical problems.

Petroleum Engineers

Petroleum engineers explore for workable reservoirs containing oil or natural gas. When one is discovered, petroleum engineers work to achieve the maximum profitable recovery from the reservoir by determining and developing the most efficient production methods.

Because only a small proportion of the oil and gas in a reservoir will flow out under natural forces, petroleum engineers develop and use various enhanced recovery methods. These include injecting water, chemicals, or steam into an oil reservoir to force more of the oil out and horizontal drilling or fracturing to connect more of a gas reservoir to a well. Since even the best methods in use today recover only a portion of the oil and gas in a reservoir, petroleum engineers work to find ways to increase this proportion.

Branches of engineering not covered in detail here, but in which there are established college curriculums, include architectural engineering (the design of a building's internal support structure); biomedical engineering (the application of engineering to medical and physiological problems); environmental engineering (a growing discipline involved with identifying, solving, and alleviating environmental problems); and marine engineering (the design and installation of ship machinery and propulsion systems).

Engineers in each branch have knowledge and training that can be applied to many fields. Electrical and electronics engineers, for example, work in the medical, computer, missile guidance, and power distribution fields. Because there are many separate problems to solve in a large engineering project, engineers in one field often work closely with specialists in other scientific, engineering, and business occupations.

Education and Training for Engineers

A bachelor's degree in engineering from an accredited program is usually required for beginning engineering jobs. However, college graduates with degrees in a physical science or mathematics may occasionally qualify for some engineering jobs. For engineering faculty positions, graduate training is essential.

Most engineering degrees are granted in branches, such as electrical, mechanical, or civil engineering. However, engineers trained in one branch may work in another. This flexibility allows employers to meet staffing needs in new technologies and specialties where engineers are in short supply. It also allows engineers to shift to fields with better employment prospects or to fields that match their interests more closely.

In addition to the standard engineering degree, many colleges offer degrees in engineering technology, which are offered as either two- or four-year sequences. These programs prepare students for practical design and production work rather than for jobs that require more theoretical, scientific, and mathematical knowledge. Graduates of four-year technology programs may get jobs similar to those obtained by graduates with bachelor's degrees in engineering. Some employers regard their skills as between those of a technician and an engineer.

Many engineers obtain graduate degrees in engineering or business administration to learn new technology, broaden their education, and enhance promotion opportunities; others obtain law degrees and become attorneys. In numerous cases, high-level executives in government and industry began their careers as engineers.

About 340 colleges and universities offer a bachelor's degree in engineering, and approximately 300 colleges offer a bachelor's degree in engineering technology, although not all are accredited programs. Although most institutions offer programs in the larger branches of engineering, only a few offer some of the smaller specialties. Also, programs of the same title may vary in content. For example, some emphasize industrial practices, preparing students for jobs in industry, while others are more theoretical and are better for students preparing to take graduate work. Therefore, students should investigate curricula and check accreditations carefully before selecting a college. Admissions requirements for undergraduate engineering schools include courses in advanced high school mathematics and the physical sciences.

Bachelor's degree programs in engineering are typically designed to last four years, but many students find that it takes between four and five years to complete their studies. In a typical four-year college curriculum, the first two years are spent studying basic sciences (mathematics, physics, and chemistry), introductory engineering, and the humanities, social sciences, and English. In the last two years, most courses are in engineering, usually with a concentration in one branch. For example, the last two years of an aerospace program might include courses such as fluid mechanics, heat transfer, applied aerodynamics, analytical mechanics, flight vehicle design, trajectory dynamics, and aerospace propulsion systems. Some programs offer a general engineering curriculum; students then specialize in graduate school or on the job.

A few engineering schools and two-year colleges have agreements whereby the two-year college provides the initial engineering education and the engineering school automatically admits students for their last two years. In addition, a few engineering schools have arrangements whereby a student spends three years in a liberal arts college studying pre-engineering subjects and two years in the engineering school and receives a bachelor's degree from each. Some colleges and universities offer five-year master's degree programs. Some five- or even six-year cooperative plans combine classroom study and practical work, permitting students to gain valuable experience and finance part of their education.

All fifty states and the District of Columbia require registration for engineers whose work may affect life, health, or property or who offer their services to the public. Registration generally requires a degree from an engineering program accredited by the Accreditation Board for Engineering and Technology, four years of relevant work experience, and successful completion of a state examination. Engineers may be registered in several states.

Beginning engineering graduates usually do routine work under the supervision of experienced engineers and, in larger companies, may also receive formal classroom or seminar-type training. As they gain knowledge and experience, they are assigned more difficult tasks with greater independence to develop designs, solve problems, and make decisions.

Engineers may become technical specialists or may supervise a staff or team of engineers and technicians. Some eventually become engineering managers or enter other managerial, management support, or sales jobs. Engineers should be able to work as part of a team and should be creative, analytical, and detail oriented. In addition, engineers should be able to communicate well—both orally and in writing.

Job Outlook for Engineers

Employment opportunities in engineering are expected to be good through the year 2006 because employment is expected to increase about as fast as the average for all occupations, while the number of degrees granted in engineering is expected to remain near present levels.

Many of the jobs in engineering are related to national defense. Because defense expenditures have declined, employment growth and job outlook for engineers may not be as strong as in times when defense expenditures were increasing. However, graduating engineers will continue to be in demand for jobs in engineering and other areas, possibly even at the same time other engineers, especially defense-industry engineers, are being laid off.

Employers will rely on engineers to further increase productivity as they increase investment in plant and equipment to expand output of goods and services. In addition, competitive pressures and advancing technology will force companies to improve and update product designs more frequently. Finally, more engineers will be needed to improve deteriorating roads, bridges, water- and pollution-control systems, and other public facilities.

Freshman engineering enrollments began declining in 1983, and the number of bachelor's degrees in engineering began declining in 1987. Although it is difficult to project engineering enrollments, this decline may continue because the total college-age population is projected to decline. Furthermore, the proportion of students interested in engineering careers has declined as prospects for college graduates in other fields have improved and interest in other programs has increased. Also, engineering schools have restricted enrollments, especially in defense-related fields such as aerospace engineering, to accommodate the reduced opportunities in defense-related industries.

Only a relatively small proportion of engineers leave the profession each year. Despite this, more than 70 percent of all job openings will arise from replacement needs. A greater proportion of replacement openings is created by engineers who transfer to management, sales, or other professional specialty occupations than by those who leave the labor force.

Most industries are less likely to lay off engineers than other workers. Many engineers work on long-term research and development projects or in activities that may continue even during recessions. In industries such as electronics and aerospace, however, large government cutbacks in defense or research and development have resulted in significant layoffs for engineers.

New computer-aided design systems have improved the design process, enabling engineers to produce or modify designs much more rapidly. Engineers now produce and analyze many more design variations before selecting a final one. However, this technology is not expected to limit employment opportunities.

It is important for engineers to continue their educations throughout their careers because much of their value to their employer depends on their knowledge of the latest technology. The pace of technological change varies by engineering specialty and industry. Engineers in high-technology areas, such as advanced electronics, may find that technical knowledge can become obsolete rapidly. Even those who continue their educations are vulnerable if the particular technology or product they have specialized in becomes obsolete. Engineers who have not kept current in their fields may find themselves passed over for promotions and are vulnerable should layoffs occur. On the other hand, it is often these high-technology areas that offer the greatest challenges, the most interesting work, and the highest salaries. Therefore, the choice of engineering specialty and employer involves an assessment not only of the potential rewards but also of the risk of technological obsolescence.

Salaries for Engineers

Starting salaries for engineers with bachelor's degrees are significantly higher than starting salaries of bachelor's degree graduates in other fields. According to the National Association of Colleges and Employers, engineering graduates with bachelor's degrees averaged about $38,500 a year in private industry in

1997; those with master's degrees and no experience, $45,400 a year; and those with doctorates, $59,200. Starting salaries for those with the bachelor's degree vary by branch:

Aerospace	$37,957
Chemical	$42,817
Civil	$33,119
Electrical	$39,513
Industrial	$38,026
Mechanical	$38,113
Metallurgical	$38,550
Mining	$36,724
Nuclear	$37,194
Petroleum	$43,674

A survey of workplaces in 160 metropolitan areas reported that beginning engineers had median annual earnings of about $34,400 in 1995, with the middle half earning between about $30,900 and $38,116 a year. Experienced midlevel engineers with no supervisory responsibilities had median annual earnings of about $59,100, with the middle half earning between about $54,000 and $65,000 a year. Median annual earnings for engineers at senior managerial levels were about $99,200.

The median annual salary for all engineers who worked full-time was about $49,200 in 1996. Those with bachelor's degrees had median annual earnings of $49,800; master's degrees, $56,700; and doctorates, $64,700. Median annual salaries for some engineering specialties were

Aerospace	$57,000
Chemical	$52,600

Civil	$46,000
Electrical	$51,700
Industrial	$43,700
Mechanical	$49,700

The average annual salary for engineers in the federal government in nonsupervisory, supervisory, and managerial positions was $61,950 in 1997.

Parade of Professionals

Meet Krista Jacobsen

Krista Jacobsen is senior systems engineer at Amati Communications Corporation in San Jose, California. She received her B.S. degree in electrical engineering from the University of Denver and both her M.S. and Ph.D. in electrical engineering from Stanford University.

"I was attracted to electrical engineering because I found those courses to be the most challenging I had ever encountered," says Jacobsen. "I worked harder than I ever had in school, and the extra effort paid off—not only did I graduate with all As in major courses, but I was awarded scholarships to an outstanding graduate school and also awarded graduate fellowships.

"While working on my Ph.D., I was employed at Amati as a consultant. When the time came to start interviewing for a post-graduation job, Amati was quick to make me an offer. I still interviewed at other companies but knew in advance that I wanted to stay because the company had been very good to me. I felt a loyalty to stay and become part of the team.

"My job is somewhat unusual and, hence, difficult to describe. The company considers me quite versatile for a Ph.D., and my employers know that I enjoy doing many difficult things, including tasks not traditionally associated with electrical engineers, such as writing and public speaking and working on heavy technical problems. My particular responsibilities include designing and managing the company's website; writing and running computer simulations to project the performance of our systems; investigating alternative solutions and design of new products; attending standards meetings (for which I write and present technical contributions); and offering technical support as necessary to the sales and marketing departments, which frequently requires travel to other companies or to conferences. On the road once or twice a month, I give presentations and/or attend meetings. At the office, I spend a lot of time writing, as ideas are useless unless they can be communicated to others. I often write internal documents explaining the problems I've been looking at and the solutions that my colleagues and I prepare.

"My advice is to work hard so you can reap the rewards. Many people drop out of engineering programs because some of the courses seem so difficult. The key is to survive the nasty courses and excel in the courses you enjoy. The road gets easier and more interesting as you progress, and eventually you'll find out that a career in engineering is fun, rewarding, and challenging."

Meet Carol Prochnow

Carol Prochnow is senior section manager at Schlumberger Well Services. She received her bachelor of science degree in electrical and computer engineering from the University of Michigan in Ann Arbor and her master of science degree in computer science from Cornell University in Ithaca, New York.

"When I was going to middle and high school, the computing profession was still in its infancy," says Prochnow. "My older brother was taking a class on the FORTRAN programming language, and I happened to look at the book and became fascinated by the whole idea of programming. I'd always loved math but didn't see a career there. Computer science, however, seemed very attractive and looked like a career that would be viable for many years.

"I am an engineering manager for about twenty people. We are responsible for the data acquisition and analysis software for a service industry called 'oil well logging,' Schlumberger's core business. When an oil company drills a well, it isn't like in movies when a huge gusher begins to spew oil into the sky. In fact, they sometimes do not know if there are hydrocarbons or where they are. Schlumberger is hired to perform a service where advanced sensors are lowered into the oil well bore, connected via a 'wife-line' conducting cable to a computer system on the surface. My section is responsible for the 'middleware' software that sit on top of this computer's operating system. This software provides data acquisition, data management, task control, and graphics facilities to support different sensors. This software is loaded into the computer system either in a truck or an offshore unit.

"A typical day is split between dealing with E-mail, having meetings, reviewing documents, and talking on the phone. Sometimes I really miss being an engineer, so I'll go in and fix some software bug. However, I consider myself pretty dangerous in getting back into the code since I do it so infrequently. But I love to build things, so I'm really glad that this is an integral part of my job.

"A day in the life of an engineer here is E-mail, Web surfing, programming and debugging, writing and reviewing documents, and attending technical meetings. We take our projects all the way from requirements analysis through delivery to our field organization.

"I would advise interested candidates to get good grades. Grades are what you need to get your foot in the door of a good job. Schlumberger engineering does not even look at resumes that have less than a B+ average.

"Continuing your education is always a plus, and internships are very valuable. In my own case, I feel that my master's degree helped me to get this job and also provided me with some skills I didn't have when I finished my undergraduate program.

"It's a good idea to work at a variety of companies during summer breaks. You'll learn a lot and also find out if you like working with the same individuals day after day. If not, engineering is probably not for you."

Meet Mary Shafer

Mary Shafer is a senior aerospace engineer for NASA at the Dryden Flight Research Center. The Dryden Flight Research Center is considered NASA's premier installation for aeronautical flight research. Located at Edward's Air Force Base in California on the Mojave Desert, the center celebrated its fiftieth anniversary in 1996. Dryden has grown from an initial group of five engineers in 1946 to a facility with more than 460 NASA government employees and about the same number of civilian contractor personnel. In addition to carrying out aeronautical research, the center also supports the space shuttle program as a primary and backup landing site and as a facility to test and validate design concepts and systems used in both development and operation.

"As a high school senior in the early sixties, I attended a National Science Foundation course at UCLA between my junior and senior years," explains Shafer. "The subject happened to be meteorology, but it gave me a chance to see that science and research provided a way to explain the world around me, which I felt was interesting and important. Then I got a summer job working for the air force, where I discovered I liked being near airplanes. I began my college career at UCLA as a chemistry major but later switched to engineering. I spent subsequent summers working for NASA and decided I truly wanted to focus my career on airplanes and flight research. And I was very lucky. I had a lot of good people to work with, a number of individuals who were willing to explain things to me and provide me with examples in everyday life that related to aerodynamics and fluid mechanics.

"During the summers at NASA, I began by reducing data, working with a ruler in engineering units, plotting the information on graph paper with orange carbon behind it. I wrote a couple of smaller programs, which impressed everybody—because at that point few people could do that. The next year I progressed to writing computer matrix manipulations designed to measure trial time stability analysis during flight. That was really interesting because it was at that point that I started to understand the rules that governed how airplanes flew.

"I earned my bachelor's degree and came back and worked another summer writing quality programs for some of the engineers. Then I went back and got my master's degree. The next summer I was writing with engineers and even married one.

"I began working as a computer programmer writing follow-up programs for the X-24B, then worked for Lockheed on the FA certification of the L-1011. I moved on to McDonnell Douglas and McDonnell Aircraft, then worked on the F-4 airplane and the initial acceptance testing of the F-15. Then I accepted a position in the air force as a systems designer working on writing programs. Finally, I came back over to NASA and got a job as a controls engineer.

"NASA employs aeronautical engineers, mechanical engineers, electrical engineers, meteorologists, and physicists. We cover a broad range of disciplines: engineering and the hard sciences, chemistry, physics, meteorology, and math. It's important that you know math and vital that you know how to program and use the computer. Also, you need to know how to write clearly and with accurate grammar. There's no point in doing research if you can't write it down clearly and concisely enough that people can understand what you did, how you did it, why you did it, and what happened when you did it. Flexibility is another important quality for researchers because you don't know how your attempts are going to come out, and you have to be able to build upon your successes or shift gears when the outcome isn't as you planned. People who are unable to deal with uncertainty may find that research is not a good field for them. And in this line of work, a robust ego is a nice thing to have.

"My projects vary, but right now, in addition to a number of small flying-qualities research projects, I'm working on one particular experiment called the aerospy. It is my responsibility to look at an airplane's various flying qualities to make sure that any modifications that are made are safe. We must fulfill our priority of being able to fly airplanes that are structurally sound.

"Most of my day is spent either talking with pilots, studying data on various computers, visiting the simulation area to see how the plane is flying, watching the input of our new ideas, or observing what the airplane looks like with the new lift, drag, or whatever the case may be. Then we put the results of our efforts in the simulator, so that the pilots can fly the planes and determine if the 'real' planes will fly as we want them to. For example, we focus on issues such as, 'Are we going to have enough runway to take off?' 'Are we going to have enough thrust?' 'Will it go forward instead of falling out of the sky?'

"My other real interest lies in how the aircraft pilot system works and what the pilot needs to get from the airplane in order to feel that it's a good airplane or a bad airplane. In his opening sentence in *Anna Karenina*, Tolstoy writes, 'All happy families are alike, but each unhappy family is unhappy in its own way.' Well, the same is true of airplanes; a good airplane is not very interesting to a quality engineer, but a bad airplane is fascinating.

"I work fairly regular hours. However, it's my understanding that this is somewhat less common in the university setting. The situation here is that we'll occasionally have a surge of work. For instance, I've got to write a paper that is due in three months, so I'll probably do that on weekends but then go back to a normal work schedule.

"Research is essentially a mutual endeavor. When you begin a project, you never really know what will be gained from your efforts, what will be gleaned, or how the new information might be used. It is only in the later stages of your work that you may be able to ascertain exactly how the information gained from your research will affect others on a grander scale. This is what provides fulfillment for all scientists and engineers—uncovering or discovering information that can benefit the world in which we live."

Meet LTC Joseph W. McVeigh

LTC Joseph W. McVeigh is chief of the operations division of the U.S. Army's Air Worthiness Qualification Test Directorate.

"I've always wanted to fly, and I decided the best way to do this was to join one of the armed services," says McVeigh. "I went to the University of Montana in Missoula because it was convenient and inexpensive (and my parents lived there). Air Force and Army ROTC were located there and were always ready to welcome a new cadet. I joined Army ROTC during my sophomore year, completed school, and received a B.S. degree in forestry in 1979. (I subsequently received an M.A. degree in computer resource management from Webster University in St. Louis, Missouri.) Once I graduated and got commissioned as a second lieutenant, I was off to Fort Knox, Kentucky, for the Army Officer's Basic Course. During the basic course, I applied for flight school and was accepted. While I was at my first flying assignment following flight school, I was selected to support an aviation test for a new type of radio. The test lasted three months, and after it was over, I realized this is what I wanted to do in the army. Although the test organization I was supporting—the Aviation Board, Ft. Rucker, Alabama—was small (thirty officers), I was lucky enough to get assigned there.

"My previous jobs include test project officer, where I conducted operational tests on several aircraft-related components, and UH-60 plans officer, where I initiated test plans for operational testing for future programs. Both of these jobs were done while I was at Fort Rucker as a captain. When I moved to the aviations systems command in St. Louis, I performed as an aeronautical engineer, working on the design of various cockpits to provide human factors input on design, layout, safety-of-flight crucial items, and so forth. My second job in St. Louis focused on performing administrative type work for two general officers. My third job was coordinating joint programs with the navy and air force so that we all worked toward using the same equipment in the future. I also worked in Canada, England, and Saudi Arabia to initiate joint laboratory type work between these countries and the army.

"The army has a small group of officers (approximately two thousand), from the rank of captain to colonel, that make up the Acquisition Corps. These officers come from all branches of the army (infantry, aviation, field artillery, and so forth). The purpose of the Acquisition Corps is to have an elite group of officers that procures all of the equipment, weapons, and vehicles that the army requires for its operations. This includes research and development, test and evaluation, program management, and staff/support functions.

"For clarification, the army differentiates between research and development (R & D) and test evaluation (T & E). I'm not sure if they are considered one and the same in the civilian world. The research and development personnel work in the army laboratories and at universities doing basic research and concept exploration. I work in the T & E area. We do the developmental testing of hardware (testing to specifications) and operational testing (testing with troops to determine operational stability)—does it work the way it's supposed to?

"Currently I'm stationed at Edwards Air Force Base with U.S. Army Airworthiness Qualification Test Directorate, where we conduct airworthiness flight testing of army helicopters and airplanes. When I first arrived, I performed as a flight test engineer, which included work on the OH-58D helicopter and the MH-47E helicopter.

"As a flight test engineer I was in charge of the flights. I told the experimental test pilot what profile to fly, how to fly it, and for how long. Designing the test plan was one of my major responsibilities. It was the road map that everyone would follow to conduct the test. I also coordinated the flight crews and crash rescue crews, test budgets, and personnel overtime.

"On a typical day as a flight test engineer, I would come in to work at 7 A.M. and pick up where I had left off on reducing data from the previous day's (or week's) flights. If a test flight was scheduled for that day for my aircraft, I briefed the crews, maintenance personnel, safety and crash rescue, and flight operations personnel on what we were doing and the schedule for the day. I would then coordinate the aircraft's preparation for the flight (if it wasn't done the previous afternoon).

"My responsibilities also included preparing the flight data card, operating all the test equipment and data recording equipment on board, and queuing the pilots as what to do next during the flight.

"If I didn't have a flight going that day but someone else did, I would fly a chase aircraft alongside them as they flew their profile (for safety). The chase pilot coordinates the airspace and makes all the radio calls to ground and air traffic control and range control.

"I remained in that job for one year and then was selected for my current position as chief of the operations division. With the people under me, I was in charge of the organization's budget, flight operations, photography and graphic arts support, technical publications support, and business office. In addition, I fly in support of flight tests here and at other remote sites that we have jurisdiction over.

"This type of career is designed for a particular type of person—one who is dedicated to his or her work and who sees things in a larger perspective, one who wants to provide the world with something better than what we already have."

Meet Ernestine Meyers

Ernestine Meyers serves as senior environmental engineer for the Division of Sanitation Facilities Construction in the Office of Environmental Health and Engineering Office of the United States Public Health Service in Albuquerque, New Mexico.

"While I was growing up, my summers were spent out in the field with my father," says Meyers. "That's how I became familiar with the inner workings of the Indian Health Service. He worked for the agency as an environmental health technician for thirty-two years. Together we traveled to different reservations where I observed what he did. I met and talked with engineers and got to know what they were responsible for. And of course, I helped whenever I could. With my father as a role model and a love for science and the outdoors, I found my career direction.

"Born on a New Mexico pueblo reservation, I am the oldest of four children. Given my choice to attend the Bureau of Indian Affairs (BIA) school or a public school in a nearby town, I decided to attend public school a few miles from the pueblo. Each day I traveled to school on a bus driven by my grandfather. Some of my friends went to BIA schools, and some went to public schools. My father attended public school, and my mother had gone to BIA. I was able to make my own choice as long as I took learning seriously. In my family, education was strongly stressed. I have always been surrounded by relatives who provided strong examples of what a quality education could render. My mother is a nurse, my uncle is an educator, another uncle is a surgeon, and many members of my extended family had gone on to earn college degrees.

"As the oldest, I was strongly urged to continue my education, so I embarked on a program that would include all the college preparatory classes I would need to ensure my entrance into a college or university. Even at the high school level, I enjoyed science and knew that would be my field of concentration.

"During the summer of my junior year in high school, I attended the Minority Introduction to Engineering course at

New Mexico State University. I was exposed to all the different types of engineering. Civil engineering easily became my choice because I always loved the outdoors. I knew I wouldn't be happy sitting at a desk or computer all the time.

"After high school, I enrolled at New Mexico State, since I had received a positive introduction to its engineering program. In addition, my uncle worked there, I had friends going to school there, and it was my home state. Happily, I was awarded a four-year Professional Guild Scholarship from the U.S. Health Service. Thus, I became a freshman there in the fall of 1979. The scholarship paid for all my undergraduate education, but in return I was obligated to work for the agency for four years upon my graduation.

"After receiving my bachelor of science degree in environmental engineering, I was assigned to the city of Tuba, Arizona, on a Navajo Indian reservation. As a field engineer, I was responsible for planning and organizing the construction of sanitation facilities and bringing in water lines for individual families. I found it to be very rewarding work, and it seems that the Navajos agreed. When I left, they presented me with an achievement medal for the work I did during those four years.

"Another of my focuses is my membership in the Commission Corps of the Public Health Service, one of the branches of the military. We have uniforms just like the navy. Upon finishing my bachelor of science degree, I had a choice of entering as a civil service employee or applying for the Commission Corps. I elected to apply for the Commission Corps because I was told that I would probably advance more quickly that way. Today I hold the rank of lieutenant commander.

"In August of 1988, I transferred to the Pacific Northwest and worked with three different tribes, assuming the same duties as I had previously. I was the only field engineer in the office, and it was kind of scary at first, but I learned to be independent. In 1991, I was selected as the engineer of the year for the Portland area.

"After three years, the Indian Health Service chose me to complete long-term training to get my master's degree in environmental engineering. The offer allowed me to go to school for one year and still receive my regular yearly salary. All educational expenses were absorbed by the agency. I felt that this was such a wonderful offer, I could not turn it down.

"I returned to New Mexico State for my advanced degree. The only hard part is that you must finish in one year, and the program is really a two-year program. It's pretty difficult to keep up, but if you are dedicated to it, you will succeed.

"Today, a typical day consists of working on the plans and designs for a pueblo springhouse, spending time with the surveyors who are doing the groundwork for some of my projects, working on specifications or proposals for future projects, dealing with contractors, or helping out the other engineers when they have any technical questions.

"My next goal is to obtain my professional registration. For this, I need to take an eight-hour exam that covers all areas of engineering. I'm sure this will not be my most pleasant experience, but it will lead to a promotion.

"The advice I would give others is to stress that you need to persevere. I was determined to get my degree no matter what. And I had some hard times in college where I thought, 'Oh, I'm not going to pass this class.'

"I used to worry about this. But I always managed to do all right. I relied on friends or sought out help from teachers. It's not easy, but nothing that's worth accomplishing ever is. Every time you reach a goal you've set for yourself, it's time to set another.

"When I went back for my master's degree (where you must maintain a B average or better), I realized I could have worked a lot harder as an undergraduate. You should always do the best you can. Just meeting minimum standards is not good enough."

Meet Cristina Calderon

Cristina Calderon serves as a transportation engineer for the city and county of San Francisco, Department of Parking and Traffic. She received her bachelor of science degree in civil engineering in 1998 from Santa Clara University in California and is registered in California as an Engineer in Training (EIT).

"My fifth grade teacher first pointed me in the direction of civil engineering after I told him I liked math and science and wanted a career that would allow me to use both subjects," says Calderon. "In high school I attended Santa Clara University's Summer Engineering Seminar and learned more about civil engineering as a major in college and as a career. In college, I concentrated on both structural and transportation engineering.

"Following college, I served as project engineer for a construction company. I chose construction because I wanted to see a project built from the ground to completion. My first project was building two hotels on the same site. One was a seven-story, reinforced concrete, post-tensioned slab hotel. The other was a four-story wood frame hotel. Overall, the project was mostly structural.

"My current job is in the transportation field. I have held it for only a short time, beginning last April. I was hired as a direct result of serving an internship there during college. Though not dangerous, at least not yet, it is highly technical and rather involved. At present, I am working on developing an Integrated Transportation Management System (ITMS) using the latest Intelligent Transportation System (ITS) technology. We are currently working on the Request for Proposal. A lot of coordination is required, and my typical day involves meetings with either consultants, the Board of Supervisors, vendors, or my own project team. The work atmosphere is often intense but comfortable, thanks to the attitudes of our team members. My average work week is forty hours, but I could easily work longer hours.

"What I like most about this job is that I am working with state of the art technology and with a great project team. What I like least is that I am often frustrated at the rate at which things occur. But we are dealing with new technology, and we don't have all the answers.

"I am a civil engineer because I like to solve problems by applying my skills in math and science as well as those derived from practical experience. I also like the challenge it provides me on a daily basis. My long-range plan, once I've gained experience in both areas of civil engineering, is to return to school, get my master's, and continue to work in design.

"My advice to other scientific types who are still in school is to gain as much experience as possible in your desired career. I particularly recommend internships and co-ops because they provide a comfortable way to decide if this is really what you wish to make your life's work. Besides, they can even lead to jobs after graduation. Mine did."

For More Information

High school students who are interested in obtaining general information on a variety of engineering disciplines should contact the Junior Engineering Technical Society by sending a self-addressed, business-size envelope with six first-class stamps affixed, to:

JETS-Guidance
1420 King Street, Suite 405
Alexandria, VA 22314
Homepage: http://www.asee.org/jets

High school students interested in obtaining information on ABET accredited engineering programs should contact:

The Accreditation Board for Engineering and Technology, Inc.
111 Market Place, Suite 1050
Baltimore, MD 21202
Homepage: http://www.abet.ba.md.us

Those wanting more detailed information should contact societies representing the individual branches of engineering. Each can provide information about careers in the particular branch.

American Institute of Aeronautics and Astronautics, Inc.
Suite 500, 1801 Alexander Bell Drive
Reston, VA 20191

American Institute of Chemical Engineers
3 Park Avenue
New York, NY 10016

American Chemical Society
Department of Career Services
1155 Sixteenth Street NW
Washington, DC 20036

American Society of Civil Engineers
1801 Alexander Bell Drive
Reston, VA 20191

Institute of Electrical and Electronics Engineers
1828 L Street NW, Suite 1202
Washington, DC 20036

Institute of Industrial Engineers, Inc.
25 Technology Park/Atlanta
Norcross, GA 30092
Homepage: http://www.iienet.org

The American Society of Mechanical Engineers
3 Park Avenue
New York, NY 10016
Homepage: http://www.asme.org

American Society of Heating, Refrigerating, and
   Air-Conditioning Engineers, Inc.
1791 Tullie Circle NE
Atlanta, GA 30329
Homepage: http://www.ashrae.org

The Minerals, Metals & Materials Society
420 Commonwealth Drive
Warrendale, PA 15086
Homepage: http://www.tms.org

ASM International
Student Outreach Program
Materials Park, OH 44073

The Society for Mining, Metallurgy, and Exploration, Inc.
P.O. Box 625002
Littleton, CO 80162

American Nuclear Society
555 North Kensington Avenue
La Grange Park, IL 60525

Society of Petroleum Engineers
P.O. Box 833836
Richardson, TX 75083

CHAPTER SIX

Careers in Computer Science and Mathematics

The new electronic interdependence recreates the world in the image of a global village. MARSHALL MCLUHAN

Mathematics possesses not only truth, but supreme beauty—a beauty cold and austere, like that of a sculpture. BERTRAND RUSSELL

C areer possibilities in the world of computers are incredibly plentiful and varied. And chronicles of success flourish. Consider perhaps the most dramatic story of all: William H. Gates III, chairperson, cofounder, and CEO of Microsoft Corporation in Redmond, Washington. By the time he was twelve, Gates was already intrigued by computers. During his high school years, he worked in the mainframe and minicomputer programming field, and in college he worked with Paul Allen to develop the BASIC programming language for the first commercially available microcomputer, the MITS Altair. He and Allen went on to form Microsoft Corporation in 1975. The company has been so successful—in part due to its top-selling Windows software and the OS/2 operating system—that, according to a *New York Times* article, more than two thousand of the company's employees are estimated to be millionaires. And Gates is reputed to be the wealthiest man in America. Even today, Gates remains actively involved in product development at Microsoft.

If your inquiring mind leans towards the world of computers and computer science—read on.

Computer Scientists and Systems Analysts

The rapid spread of computers and computer-based technologies over the past two decades has generated a need for skilled, highly trained workers to design and develop hardware and software systems and to incorporate these advances into new or existing systems. Although many narrow specializations have developed and no uniform job titles exist, this professional specialty group is widely referred to as computer scientists—a category that includes computer engineers, database administrators, computer support analysts, and systems analysts.

Computer scientists generally design computers, conduct research to improve design or use, and develop and adapt principles for applying computers to new uses. They perform many of the same duties as other computer professionals throughout a normal workday, but their jobs are distinguished by the higher level of theoretical expertise and innovation they apply to problems and the creation or application of new technology.

Computer scientists employed by academic institutions work in areas ranging from theory to hardware to language design. Some work on multidiscipline projects, developing and advancing uses for virtual reality. Their counterparts in private industry apply theory, develop specialized languages, or design programming tools, knowledge-based systems, or computer games.

Computer engineers work with the hardware and software aspects of systems design and development. Computer engineers may often work as part of a team that designs new computing devices or computer-related equipment. Software engineers design and develop both packaged and systems software.

Database administrators work with database management systems software. They reorganize and restructure data to better suit the needs of users. They also may be responsible for maintaining the efficiency of the database, system security, and may aid in design implementation.

Computer support analysts provide assistance and advice to users, interpreting problems and providing technical support for hardware, software, and systems. They may work within an organization or directly for the computer or software vendor.

Systems analysts use their knowledge and skills in a problem-solving capacity, implementing the means for computer technology to meet the individual needs of an organization. They study business, scientific, or engineering data processing problems and design new solutions using computers. This process may include planning and developing new computer systems or devising ways to apply existing systems to operations still completed manually or by some less efficient method. Systems analysts may design entirely new systems, including both hardware and software, or add a single new software application to harness more of the computer's power. They work to help an organization realize the maximum benefit from its investment in equipment, personnel, and business processes.

Analysts begin an assignment by discussing the data processing problem with managers and users to determine its exact nature. Much time is devoted to clearly defining the goals of the system and understanding the individual steps used to achieve them so that the problem can be broken down into separate programmable procedures. Analysts then use techniques such as structured analysis, data modeling, information engineering, mathematical model building, sampling, and cost accounting to plan the system. Analysts must specify the files and records to be accessed by the system and design the processing steps, as well as the format for the output that will meet the users' needs. Once the design has been developed, systems analysts prepare charts and diagrams that describe it in terms that managers and other users can understand. They may prepare a cost-benefit and return-on-investment analysis to help management decide whether the proposed system will be satisfactory and financially feasible.

When a system is accepted, systems analysts may determine what computer hardware and software will be needed to set up the system or implement changes to it. They coordinate tests and observe initial use of the system to ensure it performs as planned. They prepare specifications, work diagrams, and structure charts for computer programmers to follow and then work with them to "debug," or eliminate errors from the system.

Some organizations do not employ programmers; instead, a single worker called a programmer-analyst is responsible for both systems analysis and programming. As this becomes more commonplace, analysts will increasingly work with Computer Aided Software Engineering (CASE) tools and object-oriented programming languages, as well as client/server applications development and multimedia and Internet technology.

One obstacle associated with expanding computer use is the inability of different computers to communicate with each other. Many systems analysts are involved with connecting all the computers in an individual office, department, or establishment. This "networking" has many variations and may be referred to as local area networks, wide area networks, or multiuser systems, for example. A primary goal of networking is to allow users of microcomputers, also known as personal computers or PCs, to retrieve data from a mainframe computer and use it on their machines. This connection also allows data to be entered into the mainframe from the PC.

Because up-to-date information (accounting records, sales figures, or budget projections, for example) is so important in modern organizations, systems analysts may be instructed to make the computer systems in each department compatible so that facts and figures can be shared. Similarly, electronic mail requires open pathways to send messages, documents, and data from one computer "mailbox" to another across different equipment and program lines. Analysts must design the gates in the hardware and software to allow free exchange of data, custom applications, and the computer power to process it all. They study the seemingly incompatible pieces and create ways to link them so that users can access information from any part of the system.

A growing number of computer scientists and systems analysts are employed on a temporary or contract basis, or as consultants. For example, a company installing a new computer system may need the services of several systems analysts just to get the system running. Because not all of them would be needed once the system is functioning, the company might contract directly with the systems analysts themselves or with a temporary help agency or consulting firm. Such jobs may last from several months up to a period of two years or more.

Mathematicians

Mathematicians create new mathematical theories and techniques involving the latest technology. They solve economic, scientific, engineering, and business problems using mathematical knowledge and computational tools.

Mathematical work falls into two broad classes: theoretical (pure) mathematics and applied mathematics. However, these classes are not sharply defined and often overlap.

Theoretical mathematicians advance mathematical science by developing new principles and new relationships between existing principles of mathematics. Although theoretical mathematicians seek to increase basic knowledge without necessarily considering its practical use, this pure and abstract knowledge has been instrumental in producing or furthering many scientific and engineering achievements.

Applied mathematicians use theories and techniques, such as mathematical modeling and computational methods, to formulate and solve practical problems in business, government, engineering, and the physical, life, and social sciences. They may analyze the mathematical aspects of computer and communications networks, the effects of new drugs on disease, the aerodynamic characteristics of aircraft, or the distribution costs or manufacturing processes of businesses. Applied mathematicians working in industrial research and development may develop or enhance mathematical methods when confronted with difficult problems. Some mathematicians, called cryptanalysts, analyze and decipher encryption systems designed to transmit national security–related information.

Mathematicians use computers extensively to analyze relationships among variables, solve complex problems, develop models, and process large amounts of data.

Much work in applied mathematics, however, is carried on by persons other than mathematicians. In fact, because mathematics is the foundation upon which many other academic disciplines are built, the number of workers using mathematical techniques is many times greater than the number actually designated as mathematicians. Engineers, computer scientists, physicists, and economists are among those who use mathematics extensively but have job titles other than mathematician. Statisticians, actuaries, and operations research analysts actually are specialists in a particular branch of mathematics.

Education and Training

Computer Scientists and Systems Analysts

There is no universally accepted way to prepare for a job as a computer professional because employers' preferences depend on the work to be done. One thing is for sure—prior work experience is very important. Many people develop advanced computer skills in other occupations where they work extensively with computers, then transfer into computer occupations. For example, an accountant may become a systems analyst specializing in accounting systems development or may move into a systems analyst job after working as computer programmer.

Employers almost always seek college graduates for computer professional positions; for some of the more complex jobs, persons with graduate degrees are preferred. Generally, a doctorate, or at least a master's degree in computer science or engineering, is required for computer scientist jobs in research laboratories or academic institutions. Some computer scientists gain sufficient experience for this type of position with only a bachelor's degree, but this is difficult. Computer engineers generally require a bachelor's degree in computer engineering, electrical engineering, or math. Computer support analysts may also need a bachelor's degree in a computer-related field, as well as significant experience working with computers, including programming skills.

For systems analyst or database administrator jobs, employers seek applicants with bachelor's degrees in computer science, information science, computer information systems, or data processing. Regardless of major, employers look for people who are familiar with programming languages and have broad knowledge of and experience with computer systems and technologies. Courses in computer programming or systems design offer good preparation. For jobs in a business environment, employers usually want systems analysts to have a background in business management or a closely related field, while a background in the physical sciences, applied mathematics, or engineering is preferred for work in scientifically oriented organizations.

Systems analysts must be able to think logically, have good communication skills, and enjoy working with ideas and people. Since they often deal with a number of tasks simultaneously, they must possess the ability to concentrate and pay close attention to detail. Although both computer scientists and systems analysts often work independently, they also may work in teams on large projects. They must be able to communicate effectively with computer personnel, such as programmers and managers, as well as with other staff who have no technical computer background.

Technological advances come so rapidly in the computer field that continuous study is necessary to keep skills and knowledge up to date. Continuing education courses are usually offered by employers, hardware and software vendors, colleges and universities, or private training institutions. Additional training may come from professional development seminars offered by professional computing societies.

The Institute for Certification of Computing Professionals offers the designation Certified Computing Professional (CCP) to those who have at least four years of work experience as a computer professional, or at least two years experience and a college degree. Candidates must pass a core examination testing general knowledge plus exams in two specialty areas or in one specialty area and two computer programming languages. The Quality Assurance Institute awards the designation Certified Quality Analyst (CQA) to those who meet education and experience requirements, pass an exam, and endorse a code of ethics. Neither designation is mandatory, but professional certification may provide a job seeker a competitive advantage.

Systems analysts may be promoted to senior or lead systems analysts after several years of experience. Those who show leadership ability may also advance to management positions, such as manager of information systems or chief information officer.

Computer engineers and scientists employed in industry may eventually advance into managerial or project leadership positions. Those employed in academic institutions can become heads of research departments or published authorities in their field. Computer professionals with several years of experience and considerable expertise in a particular area may choose to start their own computer consulting firms.

Mathematicians

A bachelor's degree in mathematics is the minimum needed for prospective mathematicians. In the federal government, entry-level candidates need a four-year degree with a major in mathematics or a four-year degree with the equivalent of a mathematics major (twenty-four semester hours of mathematics courses).

In private industry, job candidates generally need master's or doctoral degrees to obtain jobs as mathematicians. Most of the positions designated for mathematicians are in research and development labs as part of technical teams. These research scientists engage in either pure mathematical research or in applied research focusing on developing or improving specific products or processes. The majority of bachelor's and master's degree holders in private industry work not as mathematicians but in related fields, such as computer science, where they are called computer programmers, systems analysts, or systems engineers.

A bachelor's degree in mathematics is offered by most colleges and universities. Mathematics courses usually required for this degree are calculus, differential equations, and linear and abstract algebra. Additional course work might include probability theory and statistics, mathematical analysis, numerical analysis, topology, modern algebra, discrete mathematics, and mathematical logic. Many colleges and universities urge or even require students majoring in mathematics to take several courses in a field that uses or is closely related to mathematics, such as computer science, engineering, operations research, physical science, statistics, or economics. A double major in mathematics and another discipline, such as computer science, economics, or one of the sciences, is particularly desirable. A prospective college mathematics major should take as many mathematics courses as possible while in high school.

About 240 colleges and universities offer a master's degree as the highest degree in either pure or applied mathematics; about two hundred offer a doctorate in pure or applied mathematics. In graduate school, students conduct research and take advanced courses, usually specializing in a subfield of mathematics. Areas of concentration include algebra, number theory, real or complex analysis, geometry, topology, logic, and applied mathematics.

If you are employed in applied mathematics, training in the field in which the mathematics will be used is very important. Fields in which applied mathematics is used extensively include physics, actuarial science, engineering, and operations research. Of increasing importance are computer and information science, business and industrial management, economics, statistics, chemistry, geology, life sciences, and the behavioral sciences.

Mathematicians should have substantial knowledge of computer programming because most complex mathematical computation and much mathematical modeling is done by computer.

Mathematicians need good reasoning ability and persistence in order to identify, analyze, and apply basic principles to technical problems. Communication skills are also important because mathematicians must be able to interact with others, including nonmathematicians, and discuss proposed solutions to problems.

Job Outlook

Computer Scientists and Systems Analysts

Computer scientists, computer engineers, and systems analysts are expected to be the three fastest growing occupations through the year 2006. Employment of computing professionals is expected to increase much faster than average as technology becomes more sophisticated and organizations continue to adopt and integrate these technologies, making for plentiful job openings. Growth will be driven by very rapid growth in computer and data processing services, which is projected to be the fastest growing industry. In addition, thousands of job openings will result each year from the need to replace workers who move into managerial positions or other occupations or who leave the labor force.

The demand for computer scientists and engineers is expected to rise as organizations attempt to maximize the efficiency of their computer systems. There will continue to be a need for increasingly sophisticated technological innovation. Competition will place organizations under growing pressure to use technological advances in areas such as office and factory automation, telecommunications technology, and scientific research. As the complexity of these applications grows, more computer scientists and systems analysts will be needed to design, develop, and implement the new technology.

As more computing power is made available to the individual, more computer scientists and systems analysts will be required to provide support. As users develop more sophisticated knowledge of computers, they become aware of the machine's potential and better able to suggest how computers could be used to increase their own productivity and that of the organization. Increasingly, users are able to design and implement their own applications and programs. As technology continues to advance, computer scientists and systems analysts will continue to need to upgrade their levels of skill and technical expertise, and the ability to interact with users will increase in importance.

The demand for "networking" to facilitate the sharing of information will be a major factor in the rising demand for systems analysts. Falling prices of computer hardware and software should continue to induce more small businesses to computerize their operations, further stimulating demand for these workers. In order to maintain a competitive edge and operate more cost effectively, firms will continue to demand computer professionals who are knowledgeable about the latest technologies and able to apply them to meet the needs of businesses. A greater emphasis on problem solving, analysis, and client/server environments will also contribute to the growing demand for systems analysts.

Individuals with advanced degrees in computer science should enjoy very favorable employment prospects because employers are demanding a higher level of technical expertise. College graduates with bachelor's degrees in computer science, computer engineering, information science, or information systems should also experience good prospects for employment. College graduates with majors other than computer science who have taken courses in computer programming, systems analysis, and other data processing areas, as well as training or experience in an applied field, should be able to find jobs as computer professionals. Those who are familiar with CASE tools, object-oriented and client/server programming, and multimedia technology will have an even greater advantage, as will individuals with significant networking, database, and systems experience. Employers should increasingly seek computer professionals who can combine strong programming and traditional systems analysis skills with good interpersonal and business skills.

Mathematicians

Employment of mathematicians is expected to increase more slowly than the average for all occupations through the year 2006. The number of jobs available for workers whose educational background is solely mathematics is not expected to increase significantly. Many firms engaged in civilian research and development that use mathematicians are not planning to expand their research departments much and, in some cases, may reduce them. Expected reductions in support for defense-related research and development will also affect employment of mathematicians, especially in the federal government. Those with a background in the study of a related discipline will have better job opportunities. However, as advancements in technology lead to expanding applications of mathematics, more workers with a knowledge of mathematics will be required. Many of these workers have job titles that reflect the end product of their work rather than the discipline of mathematics used in that work.

Bachelor's degree holders in mathematics are not qualified for most jobs as mathematicians. However, those with a strong background in computer science, electrical or mechanical engineering, or operations research have good opportunities in industry. Bachelor's degree holders who meet state certification requirements may become high school mathematics teachers.

Those with a master's degree in mathematics will face very strong competition for jobs in theoretical research. However, job opportunities in applied mathematics and related areas, such as computer programming, operations research, and engineering design in industry and government, will be more numerous.

Salaries

Computer Scientists and Systems Analysts

Median annual earnings of computer systems analysts and scientists who worked full-time in 1996 were about $46,300. The middle 50 percent earned between $34,00 and $59,900. The lowest 10 percent earned less than $24,800 and the highest tenth, more than $76,200. Computer scientists with advanced degrees generally earn more than systems analysts.

According to Robert Half International Inc., starting salaries in 1997 for systems analysts employed by large establishments employing more than fifty staff members ranged from $46,500 to $57,500. Salaries for those employed in small establishments ranged from $38,000 to $48,000. Starting salaries ranged from $54,000 to $67,500 for database administrators, from $36,000 to $55,000 for network administrators, and from $49,000 to $67,500 for software development specialists.

Starting salaries for computer scientists or computer engineers with bachelor's degrees can be significantly higher than starting salaries of bachelor's degree graduates in many other fields. According to the National Association of Colleges and Employers, starting salary offers for graduates with bachelor's degrees in computer engineering averaged $39,722 a year in 1997; those with master's degrees, $44,734 a year; and those with doctorates, $63,367. Starting offers in 1997 for graduates with bachelor's degrees in computer science averaged $36,597 a year; in information sciences, $35,407 a year; and in systems analysis, about $43,800 a year. Offers for those with bachelor's degrees vary by functional area for all types of employers, as shown in the following tabulation.

Computer programming	$35,167
Information systems	$34,689
Systems analysis and design	$36,261
Software design and development	$39,190
Hardware design and development	$41,237

In the federal government, the entrance salary for systems analysts who are recent college graduates with bachelor's degrees was about $19,520 a year in 1997; for those with superior academic records, $24,100. The average yearly salary for computer engineers in the federal government in nonsupervisory, supervisory, and managerial positions was $62,900 in early 1997.

Mathematicians

According to a 1997 survey by the National Association of Colleges and Employers, starting salary offers for mathematics graduates with bachelor's degrees averaged about $31,800 per year and for those with master's degrees, $38,300.

In the federal government in 1997, the average annual salary for mathematicians in supervisory, nonsupervisory, and managerial positions was $62,000; for mathematical statisticians, $65,660; and for cryptanalysts, $56,160.

Benefits for mathematicians tend to be similar to those offered to most professionals who work in office settings: vacation and sick leave, health and life insurance, and a retirement plan, among others.

Parade of Professionals

Meet Steven Brent Assa

Steven Assa is a research scientist. He earned his B.A. in mathematics and Scandinavian literature and his Ph.D. in mathematics from Ohio State University.

"I have known since I was a child that I would be a scientist," says Assa. "When I was very small, I thought that meant that I would be a medical doctor (psychiatrist to be exact). I held that belief until I got to college and discovered that what I really liked was mathematics and Scandinavian literature (Ibsen and Strindberg). Mathematics appealed to me because I thought that God spoke to people through universal laws conveyed in goodness and love, through mathematical equations. Understanding these equations was the same as understanding the way the world is, which is a first step to accepting the beings in the world.

"My current job is the most wonderful job that I can imagine. I may sound over the top on this, but over the past five years I have begun to see the beauty of mathematics in the physics applications that I work on at a level that makes me honored to think that I understand even a small part of their beauty and organic purpose.

"I spend about eight hours at my office and many additional hours thinking about the meaning and elegance of the equations that I manipulate. My job is to build a 3-D geometry modeling system for geological applications. I work with geologists, physicists, computer scientists, and other mathematicians. There are never enough hours in the day for me to talk to all the people that I interact with.

"My typical day begins with answering mail and checking in with a junior colleague with whom I am working very closely. If he or I have questions regarding the previous day's collaboration, we review them. Otherwise, we decide what aspect of the project to consider, decide who looks at which issues, then separate for a few hours. I make notes, decide how to approach my projects, and then close my door and get immersed. Interruptions break my concentration, but part of the fun of this job is receiving new issues from users of the computer system that I have built.

"The work is very pleasant, but I do get mentally tired from the heavy mental exertion of this work. When this happens, I pull down one of the 'classical' mathematical physics books that I have, to gain a sense of clarity and to give myself a chance to avoid my immediate problems for a few minutes.

"In a sentence, I have a job that permits me to be a permanent graduate student research assistant, with myself as the boss.

"Most of all, I like the idea that I am able to propose the majority of my work. However, my work is not open-ended—far from it. I work on projects that have a very visible payoff for my company, but I am able to focus on the parts that are exciting to me. I am trusted and have the respect of my management. I have no managerial urge, and the company has not tried to force me into this level.

"The least agreeable part of what I do is to make certain that I am not drafted back into the day-to-day engineering ranks of the company. I did this for about nine years, and it was certainly good training in general computer systems design, product completion, and group effort, but today I need time to dream. Fortunately, after my first patent was issued, the company realized that my talents could be used more efficiently in my present position.

"I recommend that you never lose your need to understand why things are the way they are. Talk to other people about your ideas and spend your time trying to make something useful out of these ideas. Read, read, read—especially the classics. Clarity of thought is timeless and independent of the problem addressed."

Meet Brian Killen

Brian Killen is a software engineer. He earned his bachelor of science degree in computer science from Kansas State University.

"I became interested in computers while in high school," reveals Killen. "And during college I served in an internship with a computer services organization. Further, I have enhanced my expertise by attending numerous seminars—anything to do with software engineering development. I have always wanted to develop products that help people communicate with each other.

"On the job, our days are influenced by the projects we are working on at the time. The projects run on one- to two-year cycles. In the beginning of a project, there is a lot of thinking, designing, and talking to customers. The latter half of a project is spent sitting at the keyboard and writing code all day. (I would say 50 percent of the project is spent writing code.) The last five months of a project are the busiest and most stressful.

"Our work atmosphere is extremely casual. I work in an office where the set hours are Monday through Friday from 8:30 A.M. until 5 P.M. However, the truth is that I usually work fifty to sixty hours per week. During crunch time, it can be seventy hours per week. It's a very intense job, definitely not low-key. The staff convenes weekly meetings via teleconference as some working on the projects are in California and India.

"What I like best in my job is creating products for people. What I like least is the turnaround time for a product. It takes two years to see results—to feel the full gratification of the job.

"In order to serve in this position effectively, you need experience in design user interfaces, software engineering skills, programming skills—networking, protocol development, C++ language—patience, the capacity to work in a team, the ability to keep the customer in mind, the skills to work well with a diverse group of people, good communication and interpersonal habits, attention to detail, stamina to work on a project for years, persistence, and insight into where the industry is going.

"You really have to like this kind of work to do this job because it's quite demanding. Long, difficult, stressful hours are fairly common. I'd advise others to obtain as much experience as early as possible because this isn't a job you are really able to understand in college. It's a job you learn by doing. Once you experience the doing, you'll be able to determine if this is something that you truly want to make your life's work."

Meet Celeste M. Combs

Celeste Combs is a human factors engineer for Microsoft. She earned her bachelor of arts degree in health education/kinesiology from the University of North Iowa, Cedar Falls, and attended the master of science program at the University of Oregon in Eugene (biomechanics) and the master of science program at the University of Washington in Seattle (bioengineering).

"I was attracted to the profession because I was focused on improving the lives of others," says Combs. "I had also been fascinated by human movement and performance most of my life. Biomechanics is science that applies physiology and mechanics to understanding movement. This helps improve performance and limits injury. However, I personally look at human beings as interacting within larger systems that not only encompass the physical realm but cognitive and emotional areas. I envisioned working in a rewarding environment with a mission to optimize all these elements. In my current position at Microsoft, I feel fortunate to work within interdisciplinary teams to reach this larger goal of optimizing the systems within which we live and spend our time daily.

"Every work experience, including interacting with colleagues, has influenced my career path. The first year or so out of college, I worked in a business environment, which was where I thought I wanted to be. However, I was really reacting to outside pressures rather than following my heart. Nevertheless, the time proved valuable because I gained some applicable business skills that would later translate to any profession.

"I changed paths and decided to pursue physiology, gaining the valuable foundation needed for my current environment and graduate work. For five years before attending graduate school, I worked for three employers; the jobs included a stint as a physical therapy assistant, another as a research assistant at the internationally renowned Institute for Aerobics Research in Dallas, and finally as research assistant in the research division of a pharmaceutical firm conducting and managing research projects around the country. All environments were beneficial and gave me experience and interaction with outstanding scientists and researchers. The cumulative experience of these positions provided me with the edge and insight required to do outstanding research and design work at Microsoft with an emphasis in human factors engineering.

"On a daily basis, I conduct biomechanical and design-related research to improve the hardware products, such as the mouse, keyboard, and gaming products, in order to optimize them from both a physical and mechanical basis. I interact with industrial designers, ergonomists, software engineers, mechanical and electrical engineers, and program managers. This position requires good communication and writing skills. Each product brings different challenges; however, my experience brings cumulative expertise to each situation.

"Like many jobs, there are deadlines, decisions, and generally very busy days. Within that context, I enjoy my job tremendously. I believe that in order to work in these environments, one must enjoy what he or she does and be able to see a broader picture. When I see a product in someone's hand or hear some positive feedback, I feel richly rewarded.

"I would advise potential scientific types to get some experience so that you are sure that this is the profession for you. That's your first challenge. Once this has been established, I would stress that you have an open mind to alternatives.

"Remember that out of every rejection or negative situation, there are many alternatives and positive situations. So it helps to be flexible. Education and knowledge are always a part of a process. You must realize that success won't come at once, but slowly through experience and time. But you should always seek the courage to live your passion—whatever inspires and motivates you most."

Meet Tom Teska

Tom Teska, a computer consultant, has worked in that capacity since 1980 and as a Certified Network Engineer since 1991.

"I earned a bachelor of science degree in computer science from the University of Wisconsin in Madison," says Teska. "I also received training on Netware 4.x administration and design and took a class on teaching Novell courses.

"My father opened a ComputerLand store in 1980. When we brought the computers in for his original stock, I started using them and discovered that I loved working on them and making them do things that no one else could do. From there, I went to helping people use them better. The consulting work lets me do this and work on computers—the best of both worlds.

"Over the years, my job has changed many times. When I worked in the commercial sector, I operated at a very high pace. My work with ComputerLand and Entre stores had me supporting upwards of a thousand companies with tens of thousands of people. I was typically working sixty to eighty hours a week for months on end.

"As a consultant and support person, the thing I like most is being able to get people's PCs to do things that no one else can do. People call me when they've got a problem that they haven't been able to solve, and I fix it for them. It makes me feel good to help them like that, and I enjoy the thanks I get from the users in those situations. I also look forward to the actual work with the computers. I have fun while I'm working.

"Presently, I am employed by a long-term contract consulting firm, and the pace is steady but not overwhelming. I report to only one client supporting fewer than ten thousand people and now work a standard forty-hour week. When I was assigned to commercial stores, there was no such thing as a typical day. That was actually one of the things I liked about it. I supported people in many different industries as well as our internal staff. One day I'd be working with bankers, and the next day I'd be helping teachers in an elementary school. Now that I support only one company, I do have typical days. I work in a cubicle with several other support people. We install and support applications and maintain the large WAN that is installed here. I also work on the second-level help desk, which means that I get the problem calls that the first-level people can't solve.

"When I worked in the commercial part of this field, I also got to work with cutting-edge technology. It was really enjoyable to work on new systems that no one had tried before. I find it particularly pleasurable to learn new things.

"My least favorite aspect of this business is having to solve the same problems over and over. Another minor annoyance is that every once in a while I run into a customer who isn't satisfied, no matter what I do for him or her. Luckily, this doesn't happen very often. Most of the time, people are very appreciative of my knowledge and my efforts.

"I feel that the most important thing about being a consultant is to keep learning. I think it's my job to know more about PCs, networks, and software than my customers. Thus, I constantly seek out new information through reading and taking classes in order to be aware of the new strategies and technologies that come to light virtually every day in this ever-changing field."

Meet Tim Lee

Tim Lee is a network consultant/LAN administrator for Anderson Consulting in Lincoln, Nebraska. He earned a bachelor of science degree in economics from Kansas State University in Manhattan, Kansas, and a master's in business adminstration from Kansas State University in Kansas City, Missouri.

"While working in mutual fund processing, I developed computer system knowledge that led to me taking this job," says Lee. "Before this, I hadn't worked in the field of computers, although they have always interested me.

"About half of my day is spent in day-to-day operations management, implementing changes to the system, finding solutions to ongoing problems. I spend about 30 percent of the day on the phone with clients, helping them solve their computer problems. The other 20 percent is spent documenting what I've done that day to help clients.

"In order to serve in this position, you need to have good problem-solving skills, PC and network experience, experience in customer service/relationship building, organizational skills, networking skills, and the ability to work in a team setting.

"Our company maintains an open-door policy. We perform our work at the client's site, so it's not exactly a casual setting. Our most hectic times are when the computer goes down or when new programs are being implemented. I work an average of forty to fifty hours per week, including some evenings.

"What I like best about this job is having the freedom to do what is best for the client. Management really encourages us to be creative with our ideas. We work very much in a team setting, which is nice. My boss is very good at hands-off management style. He trusts me to do what is best for the client. There is a strong entrepreneurial spirit here. I dislike working under the constraints of a state budget, as funds are limited, but on the positive side, it presents challenges in offering the customer the most for the money that is available.

"I'd advise prospective candidates to learn as much as you can about computer software and systems. It's important to develop great problem-solving and customer-relations skills. You have to be a people person. Gain experience as you study. Always keep in mind that your experience will help you in the future."

For More Information

Additional information about computer careers is available from:

Association for Computing (ACM)
1515 Broadway
New York, NY 10036

IEEE Computer Society
Headquarters Office
1730 Massachusetts Avenue NW
Washington, DC 20036

Information about the designation Certified Computing Professional is available from:

Institute for Certification of Computing Professionals (ICCP)
2200 East Devon Avenue, Suite 268
Des Plaines, IL 60018
Homepage: http://www.iccp.org

Information about the designation Certified Quality Analyst is available from:

Quality Assurance Institute
7575 Dr. Phillips Boulevard, Suite 350
Orlando, FL 32819

For more information about the field of mathematics, including career opportunities and professional training, contact:

American Mathematical Society
Department of Professional Programs and Services
P.O. Box 6248
Providence, RI 02940

Mathematical Association of America
1529 Eighteenth Street NW
Washington, DC 20036

For a resource guide on careers in mathematical sciences, contact:

Conference Board of the Mathematical Sciences
1529 Eighteenth Street NW
Washington, DC 20036

For specific information on careers in applied mathematics, contact:

Society for Industrial and Applied Mathematics
3600 University City Science Center
Philadelphia, PA 19104

Information on obtaining a mathematician position with the federal government may be obtained from the Office of Personnel Management through a telephone-based system. Consult your telephone directory under U.S. Government for a local number or visit the website at http://www.usajobs.opm.gov.

About the Author

J an Goldberg's love for the printed page began well before her second birthday. Regular visits to the book bindery where her grandfather worked produced a magic combination of sights and smells that she carries with her to this day.

Childhood was filled with composing poems and stories, reading books, and playing library. Elementary and high school included an assortment of contributions to school newspapers. While a full-time college student, Goldberg wrote extensively as part of her job responsibilities in the College of Business Administration at Roosevelt University in Chicago. After receiving a degree in elementary education, she was able to extend her love of reading and writing to her students.

Goldberg has written extensively in the occupations area for General Learning Corporation's *Career World Magazine*, as well as for the many career publications produced by CASS Communications. She has also contributed to a number of projects for educational publishers, including Capstone Publishing, Publications International, Scott Foresman, Addison-Wesley, and Camp Fire Boys and Girls. She is coauthor of the revised and updated edition of *Perfectionism: What's Bad About Being Too Good?*

As a feature writer, Goldberg's work has appeared in *Parenting Magazine*, *Today's Chicago Woman*, *Opportunity Magazine*, *Chicago Parent*, *Correspondent*, *Opportunity Magazine*, *Successful Student*, *Complete Woman*, *North Shore Magazine*, and the Pioneer Press newspapers. In all, she has published more than 350 pieces as a full-time freelance writer.

In addition to *Careers for Scientific Types and Others with Inquiring Minds*, she is the author of more than a dozen books published by NTC/Contemporary Publishing Group, Inc.